The Wedding Ring

A Series of Discourses for Husbands and Wives and Those Contemplating Matrimony

T. De Witt Talmage

THE CHOICE OF A WIFE

"Is there never a woman among the daughters of thy brethren, or among all my people, that thou goest to take a wife of the uncircumcised Philistines?"—JUDGES 14:3.

Samson, the giant, is here asking consent of his father and mother to marriage with one whom they thought unfit for him. He was wise in asking their counsel, but not wise in rejecting it. Captivated with her looks, the big son wanted to marry a daughter of one of the hostile families, a deceitful, hypocritical, whining, and saturnine creature, who afterward made for him a world of trouble till she quit him forever. In my text his parents forbade the banns, practically saying: "When there are so many honest and beautiful maidens of your own country, are you so hard put to for a lifetime partner that you propose conjugality with this foreign flirt? Is there such a dearth of lilies in our Israelitish gardens that you must wear on your heart a Philistine thistle? Do you take a crabapple because there are no pomegranates? Is there never a woman among the daughters of thy brethren, or among all my people, that thou goest to take a wife of the uncircumcised Philistines?"

BEAUTIFUL JEWESSES.

Excuseless was he for such a choice in a land and amid a race celebrated for female loveliness and moral worth, a land and a race of which self-denying Abigail, and heroic Deborah, and dazzling Miriam, and pious Esther, and glorious Ruth, and Mary, who hugged to her heart the blessed Lord, were only magnificent specimens. The midnight folded in their hair, the lakes of liquid beauty in their eye, the gracefulness of spring morning in their posture and gait, were only typical of the greater brilliance and glory of their soul. Likewise excuseless is any man in our time who makes lifelong alliance with any one who, because of her disposition, or heredity, or habits, or intellectual vanity, or *moraltwistification*, may be said to be of the Philistines.

MODERN FEMALE LOVELINESS.

The world never owned such opulence of womanly character or such splendor of womanly manners or multitudinous instances of wifely, motherly, daughterly, sisterly devotion, as it owns to-day. I have not words to express my admiration for good womanhood. Woman is not only man's equal, but in affectional and religious nature, which is the best part of us, she is seventy-five per cent his superior. Yea, during the last twenty years, through the increased opportunity opened for female education, the women of the country are better educated than the majority of men; and if they continue to advance in mentality at the present ratio, before long the majority of men will have difficulty in finding in the opposite sex enough ignorance to make appropriate consort. If I am under a delusion as to the abundance of good womanhood abroad, consequent upon my surroundings since the hour I entered this life until now, I hope the delusion will last until I embark from this planet. So you will understand, if I say in this course of sermons something that seems severe, I am neither cynical nor disgruntled.

NO NEED TO MARRY A FOOL.

There are in almost every farmhouse in the country, in almost every home of the great town, conscientious women, worshipful women, self-sacrificing women, holy women, innumerable Marys, sitting at the feet of Christ; innumerable mothers, helping to feed Christ in the person of His suffering disciples; a thousand capped and spectacled grandmothers Lois, bending over Bibles whose precepts they have followed from early girlhood; and tens of thousands of young women that are dawning upon us from school and seminary, that are going to bless the world with good and happy homes, that shall eclipse all their predecessors, a fact that will be acknowledged by all men except those who are struck through with moral decay from toe to cranium; and more inexcusable than the Samson of the text is that man who, amid all this unparalleled munificence of womanhood, marries a fool. But some of you are abroad suffering from such disaster, and to halt others of you from going over the same precipice, I cry out in the words of my text: "Is there never a woman among the daughters of thy brethren, or among all my people, that thou goest to take a wife of the uncircumcised Philistines?"

MARRIAGE NOT FOR ALL.

That marriage is the destination of the human race is a mistake that I want to correct before I go further. There are multitudes who never will marry, and still greater multitudes who are not fit to marry. In Great Britain to-day there are nine hundred and forty-eight thousand more women than men, and that, I understand, is about the ratio in America. By mathematical and inexorable law, you see, millions of women will never marry. The supply for matrimony is greater than the demand, the first lesson of which is that every woman ought to prepare to take care of herself if need be. Then there are thousands of men who have no right to marry, because they have become so corrupt of character that their offer of marriage is an insult to any good woman. Society will have to be toned up and corrected on this subject, so that it shall realize that if a woman who has sacrificed her honor is unfitted for marriage, so is any man who has ever sacrificed his purity. What right have *you, O masculine beast*! whose life has been loose, to take under your care the spotlessness of a virgin reared in the sanctity of a respectable home? Will a buzzard dare to court a dove?

THE FIRST STEP.

But the majority of you will marry, and have a right to marry, and as your religious teacher I wish to say to these men, in the choice of a wife first of all seek divine direction. About thirty-five years ago, when Martin Farquhar Tupper, the English poet, urged men to prayer before they decided upon matrimonial association, people laughed. And some of them have lived to laugh on the other side of their mouth.

EMINENT BLUNDERERS.

The need of divine direction I argue from the fact that so many men, and some of them strong and wise, have wrecked their lives at this juncture. Witness Samson and this woman of Timnath! Witness *Socrates*, pecked of the historical Xantippe! Witness *Job*, whose wife had nothing to prescribe for his carbuncles but allopathic doses of profanity! Witness *Ananias*, a liar, who might perhaps have been cured by a truthful spouse, yet marrying as great a liar as himself—Sapphira! Witness *JohnWesley*, one of the best men that ever lived, united to one of the most outrageous and scandalous of women, who sat in City Road Chapel, making mouths at him while he preached! Witness the once connubial wretchedness of *John Ruskin*, the great art essayist, and *FrederickW.Robertson*, the great preacher! Witness a thousand

HELLS ON EARTH

kindled by unworthy wives, termagants that scold like a March north-easter; female spendthrifts, that put their husbands into fraudulent schemes to get money enough to meet the lavishment of domestic expenditure; *opium-using women*—about four hundred thousand of them in the United States—who will have the drug, though it should cause the eternal damnation of the whole household; heartless and overbearing, and namby-pamby and unreasonable women, yet married—married perhaps to good men! These are the women who build the low club-houses, where the husbands and sons go because they can't stand it at home. On this sea of matrimony, where so many have been wrecked, am I not right in advising divine pilotage?

NUMEROUS PITFALLS.

Especially is devout supplication needed, because of the fact that society is so full of artificialities that men are deceived as to whom they are marrying, and no one but the Lord knows. After the dressmaker, and the milliner, and the jeweler, and the hair-adjuster, and the dancing-master, and the cosmetic art have completed their work, how is an unsophisticated man to decipher the physiological hieroglyphics, and make accurate judgment of who it is to whom he offers hand and heart? This is what makes so many recreant husbands. They make an honorable marriage contract, but the goods delivered are so different from the sample by which they bargained. They were simply swindled, and they backed out. They mistook Jezebel for Longfellow's Evangeline, and Lucretia Borgia for Martha Washington.

Aye, as the Indian, chief boasts, of the scalps he has taken, so there are in society to-day many coquettes who boast of the masculine hearts they have captured. And these women, though they may live amid richest upholstery, are not so honorable as the cyprians of the street, for these advertise their infamy, while the former profess heaven while they mean hell.

There is so much counterfeit womanhood abroad it is no wonder that some cannot tell the genuine coin from the base. Do you not realize you need divine guidance when I remind you that mistake is possible in this important affair, and, if made, is irrevocable?

A MISTAKE IRREPARABLE.

The worst predicament possible is to be unhappily yoked together. You see, it is impossible to break the yoke. The more you pull apart, the more galling the yoke. The minister might bring you up again, and in your presence read the marriage ceremony backward, might put you on the opposite sides of the altar from where you were when you were united, might take the ring off of the finger, might rend the wedding-veil asunder, might tear out the marriage leaf from the family Bible record, but all that would fail to unmarry you. It is better not to make the mistake than to attempt its correction. But men and women do not reveal all their characteristics till after marriage, and how are you to avoid committing the fatal blunder? There is only one Being in the universe who can tell you whom to choose, and that is the Lord of Paradise. He made Eve for Adam, and Adam for Eve, and both for each other. Adam had not a large group of women from whom to select his wife, but it is fortunate, judging from some mistakes which she afterward made, that it was Eve or nothing.

There is in all the world some one who was made for you, as certainly as Eve was made for Adam. All sorts of mistakes occur because Eve was made out of a rib from Adam's side. Nobody knows which of his twenty-four ribs was taken for the nucleus. If you depend entirely upon yourself in the selection of a wife, there are twenty-three possibilities to one that you will select the wrong rib. By the fate of Ahab, whose wife induced him to steal; by the fate of Macbeth, whose wife pushed him into massacre; by the fate of James Ferguson, the philosopher, whose wife entered the room while he was lecturing and willfully upset his astronomical apparatus, so that he turned to the audience and said: "Ladies and gentlemen, I have the misfortune to be married to this woman;" by the fate of Bulwer, the novelist, whose wife's temper was so incompatible that he furnished her a beautiful house near London and withdrew from her company, leaving her with the dozen dogs whom she entertained as pets; by the fate of John

Milton, who married a termagant after he was blind, and when some one called her a rose, the poet said: "I am no judge of flowers, but it may be so, for I feel the thorns daily;" by the fate of an Englishman whose wife was so determined to dance on his grave that he was buried in the sea; by the fate of a village minister whom I knew, whose wife threw a cup of hot tea across the table because they differed in sentiment—by all these scenes of disquietude and domestic calamity, we implore you to be cautious and prayerful before you enter upon the connubial state, which decides whether a man shall have two heavens or two hells, a heaven here and heaven forever, or a hell now and a hell hereafter.

NOBLE WIVES.

By the bliss of Pliny, whose wife, when her husband was pleading in court, had messengers coming and going to inform her what impression he was making; by the joy of Grotius, whose wife delivered him from prison under the pretence of having books carried out lest they be injurious to his health, she sending out her husband unobserved in one of the bookcases; by the good fortune of Roland, in Louis' time, whose wife translated and composed for her husband, while Secretary of the Interior—talented, heroic, wonderful Madame Roland; by the happiness of many a man who has made intelligent choice of one capable of being prime counsellor and companion in brightness and in grief—pray to Almighty God, morning, noon, and night that at the right time and in the right way He will send you a good, honest, loving, sympathetic wife; or if she is not sent to you, that you may be sent to her.

AVOID MATCHMAKERS.

At this point let me warn you not to let a question of this importance be settled by the celebrated matchmakers flourishing in almost every community. Depend upon your own judgment divinely illumined. These brokers in matrimony are ever planning how they can unite impecunious innocence to an heiress, or celibate woman to millionaire or marquis, and that in many cases makes life an unhappiness. How can any human being, who knows neither of the two parties as God knows them, and who is ignorant of the future, give such direction as you require at such a crisis?

Take the advice of the earthly matchmaker instead of the divine guidance, and you may some day be led to use the words of Solomon, whose experience in home life was as melancholy as it was multitudinous. One day his palace with its great wide rooms and great wide doors and great wide hall was too small for him and the loud tongue of a woman belaboring him about some of his neglects, and he retreated to the housetop to get relief from the lingual bombardment. And while there he saw a poor man on one corner of the roof with a mattress for his only furniture, and the open sky his only covering. And Solomon envies him and cries out: "It is better to dwell in the corner of the housetop than with *a brawling woman* in a wide house." And one day during the rainy season the water leaked through the roof of the palace and began to drop in a pail or pan set there to catch it. And at one side of him all day long the water went drop! drop! drop! while on the other side a female companion quarrelling about this, and quarrelling about that, the acrimonious and petulant words falling on his ear in ceaseless pelting—drop! drop! drop! and he seized his pen and wrote: "A continual dropping in a very rainy day and *a contentious woman* are alike." If Solomon had been as prayerful at the beginning of his life as he was at the close, how much domestic infelicity he would have avoided!

But prayer about this will amount to nothing unless you pray soon enough. Wait until you are fascinated and the equilibrium of your soul is disturbed by a magnetic and exquisite presence, and then you will answer your own prayers, and you will mistake your own infatuation for the voice of God.

AVOID SCOFFERS.

If you have this prayerful spirit you will surely avoid all female scoffers at the Christian religion; and there are quite a number of them in all communities. It must be told that, though the only influence that keeps woman from being estimated and treated as a slave—aye, as a brute and a beast of burden—is Christianity, since where it is not dominant she is so treated, yet there are women who will so far forget themselves and forget their God that they will go and hear lecturers malign Christianity and scoff at the most sacred things of the soul. A good woman, over-persuaded by her husband, may go once to hear such a tirade against the Christian religion, not fully knowing what she is going to hear; but she will not go twice.

A woman, not a Christian, but a respecter of religion, said to me: "I was persuaded by my husband to go and hear an infidel lecturer once, but going home, I said to him: 'My dear husband, I would not go again though my declinature should result in our divorcement forever.'" And the woman was right. If after all that Christ and Christianity have done for a woman, she can go again and again to hear such assaults, she is *an awful creature*, and you had better not come near such a reeking lepress. She needs to be washed, and for three weeks to be soaked in carbolic acid, and for a whole year, fumigated, before she is fit for decent society. While it is not demanded that a woman be a Christian before marriage, she must have regard for the Christian religion or she is a bad woman and unworthy of being your companion in a life charged with such stupendous solemnity and vicissitudes.

TWO ESSENTIAL QUALITIES.

What you want, O man! in a wife, is not a butterfly of the sunshine, not a giggling nonentity, not a painted doll, not a gossiping gadabout, not a mixture of artificialities which leave you in doubt as to where the humbug ends and the woman begins, but an earnest soul, one that cannot only laugh when you laugh, but weep when you weep. There will be wide, deep graves in your path of life, and you will both want steadying when you come to the verge of them, I tell you! When your fortune fails you will want some one to talk of treasures in heaven, and not charge upon you with a bitter, "I told you so." As far as I can analyze it, *sincerity and earnestness* are the foundation of all worthy wifehood. Get that, and you get all. Fail to get that, and you get nothing but what you will wish you never had got.

BEAUTY A BENEDICTION.

Don't make the mistake that the man of the text made in letting his eye settle the question in which coolest judgment directed by divine wisdom are all-important. He who has no reason for his wifely choice except a pretty face is like a man who should buy a farm because of the dahlias in the front dooryard. Beauty is a talent, and when God gives it He intends it as a benediction upon a woman's face. When the good *Princess of Wales* dismounted from the railtrain last summer, and I saw her radiant face, I could understand what they told me the day before, that, when at the great military hospital where are now the wounded and the sick from the Egyptian and other wars, the Princess passed through, all the sick were cheered at her coming, and those who could be roused neither by doctor nor nurse from their stupor, would get up on their elbows to look at her, and wan and wasted lips prayed an audible prayer: "God bless the Princess of Wales! Doesn't she look beautiful?"

But how uncertain is the tarrying of beauty in a human countenance! Explosion of a kerosene lamp turns it into scarification, and a scoundrel with one dash of vitriol may dispel it, or Time will drive his chariot wheels across that bright face, cutting it up in deep ruts and gullies. But there is an eternal beauty on the face of some women, whom a rough and ungallant world may criticise as homely; and though their features may contradict all the laws of Lavater on physiognomy, yet they have graces of soul that will keep them attractive for time and glorious through all eternity.

There are two or three circumstances in which the plainest wife is a queen of beauty to her husband, whatever her stature or profile. By financial panic or betrayal of business partner, the man goes down, and returning to his home that evening he says: "*I am ruined*; I am in disgrace forever; I care not whether I live or die." It is an agitated story he is telling in the household that winter night. He says: "The furniture must go, the house must go, the social position must go," and from being sought for obsequiously they must be cold-shouldered everywhere. After he ceases talking, and the wife has heard all in silence, she says: "Is that all? Why, you had nothing when I married you, and you have only come back to where you started. If you think that my happiness and that of the children depend on these trappings, you do not know me, though we have lived together thirty years. God is not dead, and the National Bank of Heaven has not suspended payment, and if you don't mind, I don't care a cent. What little we need of food and raiment the rest of our lives we can get, and I don't propose to sit down and mope and groan. Mary, hand me that darning-needle. I declare! I have forgotten to set the rising for those cakes!" And while she is busy at it he hears her humming Newton's old hymn, "To-Morrow:"

> "It can bring with it nothing
>   But He will bear us through;
> Who gives the lilies clothing
>   Will clothe His people too;
> Beneath the spreading heavens
>   No creature but is fed;
> And He who feeds the ravens
>   Will give His children bread.
>
> "Though vine nor fig-tree either
>   Their wonted fruit should bear,
> Though all the fields should wither
>   Nor flocks nor herds be there;
> Yet God the same abiding,
>   His praise shall tune my voice;
> For while in Him confiding
>   I cannot but rejoice."

The husband looks up in amazement, and says: "Well, well, you are the greatest woman I ever saw. I thought you would faint dead away when I told you." And as he looks at her, all the glories of physiognomy in the court of Louis XV. on the modern fashion plates are tame as compared with the superhuman splendors of that woman's face. Joan of Arc, Mary Antoinette, and La Belle Hamilton, the enchantment of the court of Charles II., are nowhere.

A WIFE'S DEATH.

There is another time when the plainest wife is a queen of beauty to her husband. She has done the work of life. She has reared her children for God and heaven, and though some of them may be a little wild they will yet come back, for God has promised. She is dying, and her husband stands by. They think over all the years of their companionship, the weddings and the burials, the ups and the downs, the successes and the failures. They talk over the goodness of God and His faithfulness to children's children. She has no fear about going. The Lord has sustained her so many years she would not dare to distrust Him now. The lips of both of them tremble as they say good-bye and encourage each other about an early meeting in a better world. The breath is feebler and feebler, and stops. Are you sure of it? Just hold that mirror at the mouth, and see if there is any vapor gathering on the surface. Gone! As one of the neighbors takes the old man by the arm and gently says: "Come, you had better go into the next room and rest," he says: "Wait a moment; I must take one more look at that face and at those hands!" Beautiful! Beautiful!

My friends, I hope you do not call that death. That is an autumnal sunset. That is a crystalline river pouring into a crystal sea. That is the solo of human life overpowered by hallelujah chorus. That is a queen's coronation. That is heaven. That is the way my father stood at eighty-two, seeing my mother depart at seventy-nine. Perhaps so your father and mother went. I wonder if we shall die as well?

THE CHOICE OF A HUSBAND.ToC

"The Lord grant you that ye may find rest, each of you in the house of her husband."—Ruth 1:9.

This was the prayer of pious Naomi for Ruth and Orpah, and is an appropriate prayer now in behalf of unmarried womanhood. Naomi, the good old soul, knew that the devil would take their cases in hand if God did not, so she prays: "The Lord grant you that ye may find rest, each of you in the house of her husband."

In this series of sermons on "The Wedding Ring" I last Sabbath gave prayerful and Christian advice to men in regard to the selection of a wife, and to-day I give the same prayerful and Christian advice to women in regard to the selection of a husband, but in all these sermons saying much that I hope will be appropriate for all ages and all classes.

VOLUNTARY CELIBACY.

I applaud the celibacy of a multitude of women who, rather than make unfit selection, have made none at all. It has not been a lack of opportunity for marital contract on their part, but their own culture and refinement, and their exalted idea as to what a husband ought to be, have caused their declinature. They have seen so many women marry imbeciles, or ruffians, or incipient sots, or life-time incapables, or magnificent nothings, or men who before marriage were angelic and afterward diabolic, that they have been alarmed and stood back. They saw so many boats go into the maelstrom that they steered into other waters. Better for a woman to live alone, though she live a thousand years, than to be annexed to one of these masculine failures with which society is surfeited. The patron saint of almost every family circle is some such unmarried woman, and among all the families of cousins she moves around, and her coming in each house is the morning, and her going away is the night.

A BENEFICENT SPINSTERHOOD.

In my large circle of kindred, perhaps twenty families in all, it was an Aunt Phœbe. Paul gave a letter of introduction to one whom he calls "Phœbe, our sister," as she went up from Cenchrea to Rome, commending her for her kindness and Christian service, and imploring for her all courtesies. I think Aunt Phœbe was named after her. Was there a sickness in any of the households, she was there ready to sit up and count out the drops of medicine. Was there a marriage, she helped deck the bride for the altar. Was there a new soul incarnated, she was there to rejoice at the nativity. Was there a sore bereavement she was there to console. The children, rushed out at her first appearance, crying, "Here comes Aunt Phœbe," and but for parental interference they would have pulled her down with their caresses—for she was not very strong, and many severe illnesses had given her enough glimpses of the next world to make her heavenly-minded. Her table was loaded up with Baxter's "Saints' Rest," Doddridge's "Rise and Progress," and Jay's "Morning and Evening Exercises," and John Bunyan's "Pilgrim's Progress," and like books, which have fitted out whole generations for the heaven upon which they have already entered.

A GLIMPSE OF HEAVEN.

"De Witt," she said to me one day, "twice in my life I have been so overwhelmed with the love of God that I fainted away and could hardly be resuscitated. Don't tell me there is no heaven. I have seen it twice." If you would know how her presence would soothe an anxiety, or lift a burden, or cheer a sorrow, or leave a blessing on every room in the house, ask any of the Talmages. She had tarried at her early home, taking care of an invalid father, until the bloom of life had somewhat faded; but she could interest the young folks with some three or four tender passages in her own history, so that we all knew that it was not through lack of opportunity that she was not the queen of one household, instead of being a benediction on a whole circle of households.

At about seventy years of age she made her last visit to my house, and when she sat in my Philadelphia church I was more embarrassed at her presence than by all the audience, because I felt that in religion I had got no further than the A B C, while she had learned the whole alphabet, and for many years had finished the Y and Z. When she went out of this life into the next, what a shout there must have been in heaven, from the front door clear up to the back seat in the highest gallery! I saw the other day in the village cemetery of Somerville, N.J., her resting-place, the tombstone having on it the words which thirty years ago she told me she would like to have inscribed there, namely: "The Morning Cometh."

ILLUSTRIOUS SPINSTERS.

Had she a mission in the world? Certainly. As much as Caroline Herschel, first amanuensis for her illustrious brother, and then his assistant in astronomical calculations, and then discovering worlds for herself, dying at ninety-eight years of age, still busy with the stars till she sped beyond them; as much as had Florence Nightingale, the nurse of the Crimea; or Grace Darling, the oarswoman of the Long Stone Lighthouse; or Mary Lyon, the teacher of Mount Holyoke Female Seminary; or Hannah More, the Christian authoress of England; or Dorothea Dix, the angel of mercy for the insane; or Anna Etheridge, among the wounded of Blackburn's Fort; or Margaret Breckenridge, at Vicksburg; or Mary Shelton, distributing roses and grapes and cologne in western hospital; or thousands of other glorious women like them, who never took the marriage sacrament. Appreciate all this, my sister, and it will make you deliberate before you rush out of the single state into another, unless you are sure of betterment.

A DIFFICULT BUSINESS.

Deliberate and pray. Pray and deliberate. As I showed you in my former sermon, a man ought to supplicate Divine guidance in such a crisis; how much more important that you solicit it! It is easier for a man to find an appropriate wife than for a woman to find a good husband. This is a matter of arithmetic, as I showed in former discourse. Statistics show that in Massachusetts and New York States women have a majority of hundreds of thousands. Why this is we leave others to surmise. It would seem that woman is a favorite with the Lord, and that therefore He has made more of that kind. From the order of the creation in paradise it is evident that woman is an improved edition of man. But whatever be the reason for it, the fact is certain that she who selects a husband has a smaller number of people to select from than he who selects a wife. Therefore a woman ought to be especially careful in her choice of life-time companionship. She cannot afford to make a mistake. If a man err in his selection he can spend his evenings at the club, and dull his sensibilities by tobacco-smoke; but woman has no club-room for refuge, and would find it difficult to habituate herself to cigars. If a woman make a bad job of marital selection, the probability is that nothing but a funeral can relieve it. Divorce cases in court may interest the public, but the love-letters of a married couple are poor reading, except for those who write them. Pray God that you be delivered from irrevocable mistake!

PARTNERS TO AVOID.

Avoid affiance with a despiser of the Christian religion, whatever else he may have or may not have. I do not say he must needs be a religious man, for Paul says the unbelieving husband is sanctified by the wife; but marriage with a man who hates the Christian religion will insure you a life of wretchedness. He will caricature your habit of kneeling in prayer. He will speak depreciatingly of Christ. He will wound all the most sacred feelings of your soul. He will put your home under the anathema of the Lord God Almighty. In addition to the anguish with which he will fill your life, there is great danger that he will despoil your hope of heaven, and make your marriage relation an infinite and eternal disaster. If you have made such engagement, your first duty is to break it. My word may come just in time to save your soul.

HUSBANDS SELDOM REFORM.

Further, do not unite in marriage with a man of bad habits in the idea of reforming him. If now, under the restraint of your present acquaintance, he will not give up his bad habits, after he has won the prize you cannot expect him to do so. You might as well plant a violet in the face of a northeast storm with the idea of appeasing it. You might as well run a schooner alongside of a burning ship with the idea of saving the ship. The consequence will be, schooner and ship will be destroyed together.

The almshouse could tell the story of a hundred women who married men to reform them. If by twenty-five years of age a man has been grappled by intoxicants, he is under such headway that your attempt to stop him would be very much like running up the track with a wheelbarrow to stop a Hudson River express train. What you call an inebriate nowadays is not a victim to wine or whiskey, but to logwood and strychnine and nux vomica. All these poisons have kindled their fires in his tongue and brain, and all the tears of a wife weeping cannot extinguish the flames. Instead of marrying a man to reform him, let him reform first, and then give him time to see whether the reform is to be permanent. Let him understand that if he cannot do without his bad habits for two years he must do without you forever.

MEN WEDDED TO THE WORLD.

Avoid union with one supremely selfish, or so wound up in his occupation that he has no room for another. You occasionally find a man who spreads himself so widely over the path of life that there is no room for any one to walk beside him. He is not the one blade of the scissors incomplete without the other blade, but he is a chisel made to cut his way through life alone, or a file full of roughness, made to be drawn across society without any affinity for other files. His disposition is a lifelong protest against marriage. Others are so married to their occupation or profession that the taking of any other bride is a case of bigamy. There are men as severely tied to their literary work as was Chatterton, whose essay was not printed because of the death of the Lord Mayor. Chatterton made out the following account: "Lost by the Lord Mayor's death in this essay one pound eleven shillings and six-pence. Gained in elegies and essays five pounds and five shillings." Then he put what he had gained by the Lord Mayor's death opposite to what he had lost, and wrote under it: "And glad he is dead by three pounds thirteen shillings and six-pence." When a man is as hopelessly literary as that he ought to be a perpetual celibate; his library, his laboratory, his books are all the companionship needed.

Indeed, some of the mightiest men this world ever saw have not patronized matrimony. Cowper, Pope, Newton, Swift, Locke, Walpole, Gibbon, Hume, Arbuthnot, were single. Some of these marriage would have helped. The right kind of a wife would have cured Cowper's gloom, and given to Newton more practicability, and been a relief to Locke's overtasked brain. A Christian wife might have converted Hume and Gibbon to a belief in Christianity. But Dean Swift did not deserve a wife, from the way in which he broke the heart of Jane Waring first, and Esther Johnson afterward, and last of all "Vanessa." The great wit of the day, he was outwitted by his own cruelties.

PREDESTINATION IN MARRIAGE.

Amid so many possibilities of fatal mistake, am I not right in urging you to seek the unerring wisdom of God, and before you are infatuated? Because most marriages are fit to be made convinces us that they are divinely arranged. Almost every cradle has an affinity toward some other cradle. They may be on the opposite sides of the earth, but one child gets out of this cradle, and another child gets out of that cradle, and with their first steps they start for each other. They may diverge from the straight path, going toward the North, or South, or East, or West. They may fall down, but the two rise facing each other. They are approaching all through infancy. The one all through the years of boyhood is going to meet the one who is coming through all the years of girlhood to meet him. The decision of parents as to what is best concerning them, and the changes of fortune, may for a time seem to arrest

THE TWO JOURNEYS;

but on they go. They may never have seen each other. But the two pilgrims who started at the two cradles are nearing. After eighteen, twenty, or thirty years, the two come within sight. At the first glance they may feel a dislike, and they may slacken their step; yet something that the world calls fate, and that religion calls Providence, urges them on and on. They must meet. They come near enough to join hands in social acquaintance, after awhile to join hands in friendship, after awhile to join hearts. The delegate from the one cradle comes up the east aisle of the church with her father. The delegate from the other cradle comes up the west aisle of the church. The two long journeys end at the snow-drift of the bridal veil. The two chains made out of many years are forged together by the golden link which the groom puts upon the third finger of the left hand. One on earth, may they be one in heaven!

But there are so many exceptions to the general rule of natural affinity that only those are safe who pray for a heavenly hand to lead them. Because they depended on themselves and not on God there are thousands of women every year going to the slaughter. In India women leap on the funeral pyre of a dead husband. We have a worse spectacle than that in America—women innumerable leaping on the funeral pyre of a living husband.

THE ADVERTISING BRUTE.

Avoid all proposed alliances through newspaper advertisements. Many women, just for fun, have answered such advertisements, and have been led on from step to step to catastrophe infinite. All the men who write such advertisements are villains and lepers—all, without a single exception. All! All! Do you answer them just for fun? I will tell you a safer and healthier fun. Thrust your hand through the cage at a menagerie, and stroke the back of a cobra from the East Indies. Put your head in the mouth of a Numidian lion, to see if he will bite. Take a glassful of Paris green mixed with some delightful henbane. These are safer and healthier fun than answering newspaper advertisements for a wife.

MARRY INDEPENDENT MEN.

My advice is: Marry a man who is a fortune in himself. Houses, lands, and large inheritance are well enough, but the wheel of fortune turns so rapidly that through some investment all these in a few years may be gone. There are some things, however, that are a perpetual fortune—good manners, geniality of soul, kindness, intelligence, sympathy, courage, perseverance, industry, and whole-heartedness. Marry such a one and you have married a fortune, whether he have an income now of $50,000 a year or an income of $1000. A bank is secure according to its capital stock, and not to be judged by the deposits for a day or a week. A man is rich according to his sterling qualities, and not according to the mutability of circumstances, which may leave with him a large amount of resources to-day and withdraw them to-morrow. If a man is worth nothing but money he is poor indeed. If a man have upright character he is rich. Property may come and go, he is independent of the markets. Nothing can buy him out, nothing can sell him out. He may have more money one year than another, but his better fortunes never vacillate.

AVOID PERFECT MEN.

Yet do not expect to find a perfect man. If you find one without any faults, incapable of mistakes, never having guessed wrongly, his patience never having been perturbed, immaculate in speech, in temper, in habits, do not marry him. Why? Because you would enact a swindle. What would you do with a perfect man who are not perfect yourself? And how dare you hitch your imperfection fast on such supernatural excellence? What a companion you would make for an angel! In other words, there are no perfect men. There never was but one perfect pair, and they slipped down the banks of paradise together. We occasionally find a man who says he never sins. *We know he lies* when he says it. We have had financial dealings with two or three perfect men, and they cheated us wofully. Do not, therefore, look for an immaculate husband, for you will not find him.

PLENTY OF GOOD HUSBANDS.

But do not become cynical on this subject. Society has a great multitude of grand men who know how to make home happy. When they come to be husbands they evince a nobility of nature and a self-sacrificing spirit that surprise even the wife. These are the men who cheerfully sit in dark and dirty business offices, ten feet by twelve, in summer time hard at work while the wives and daughters are off at Saratoga, Mount Desert, or the White Sulphur. These are the men who, never having had much education themselves, have their sons at Yale, and Harvard, and Virginia University. These are the men who work themselves to death by fifty years of age, and go out to Greenwood leaving large estate and generous life-insurance provision for their families.

There are husbands and fathers here by the hundreds who would die for their households. If outlawry should ever become dominant in our cities they would stand in their doorway, and with their own arm would cleave down, one by one, fifty invaders face to face, foot to foot, and every stroke a demolition. This is what makes an army in defence in a country fight more desperately than an army of conquest. It is not so much the abstract sentiment of a flag as it is wife, and children, and home that turns enthusiasm into a fury. The world has such men by the million, and the homunculi that infest all our communities must not hinder women from appreciating the glory of true manhood.

FIDELITY IN ADVERSITY.

I was reading of a bridal reception. The young man had brought home the choice of his heart in her elaborate and exquisite apparel. As she stood in the gay drawing-room, and amid the gay group, the young man's eyes filled with tears of joy as he thought that she was his. Years passed by, and they stood at the same parlor on another festal occasion. She wore the same dress, for business had not opened as brightly to the young husband as he expected, and he had never been able to purchase for her another dress. Her face was not as bright and smooth as it had been years before, and a careworn look had made its signature on her countenance. As the husband looked at her he saw the difference between this occasion and the former, and he went over to where she sat, and said: "You remember the time when we were here before. You have the same dress on. Circumstances have somewhat changed, but you look to me far more beautiful than you did then." There is such a thing as conjugal fidelity, and many of you know it in your own homes.

But, after all the good advice we may give you, we come back to the golden pillar from which we started, the tremendous truth that no one but God can guide you in safety about this matter that may decide your happiness for two worlds, this and the next. So, my sister, I put your case where Naomi put that of Ruth and Orpah when she said: "The Lord grant you that ye may find rest, each of you in the house of her husband."

THE WEDDING.

I imagine the hour for which you pledged your troth has arrived. There is much merry-making among your young friends, but there is an undertone of sadness in all the house. Your choice may have been the gladdest and the best, and the joy of the whole round of relatives, but when a young eaglet is about to leave the old nest, and is preparing to put out into sunshine and storm for itself, it feels its wings tremble somewhat. So she has a good cry before leaving home, and at the marriage father and mother always cry, or feel like it. If you think it is easy to give up a daughter in marriage, though it be with brightest prospects, you will think differently when the day comes. To have all along watched her from infancy to girlhood, and from girlhood to womanhood, studious of her welfare, her slightest illness an anxiety, and her presence in your home an ever-increasing joy, and then have her go away to some other home—aye, all the redolence of orange-blossoms, and all the chime of marriage bells, and all the rolling of wedding march in full diapason, and all the hilarious congratulations of your friends cannot make you forget that you are suffering a loss irreparable. But you know it is all right, and you have a remembrance of an embarkation just like it twenty-five or thirty years ago, in which you were one of the parties; and, suppressing as far as possible your sadness, you say, "Good-bye."

VISIT THE OLD HOME.

I hope that you, the departing daughter, will not forget to write often home; for, whatever betide you, the old folks will never lose their interest in your welfare. Make visits to them also as often, and stay as long as you can, for there will be changes at the old place after awhile. Every time you go you will find more gray hairs on father's head and more wrinkles on mother's brow; and after awhile you will notice that the elastic step has become decrepitude. And some day one of the two pillars of your early home will fall, and after awhile the other pillar of that home will fall, and it will be a comfort to yourself if, when they are gone, you can feel that while you are faithful in your new home you never forget your old home, and the first friends you ever had, and those to whom you are more indebted than you ever can be to any one else except to God—I mean your father and mother. Alexander Pope put it in effective rhythm when he said:

> "Me let the tender office long engage
> To rock the cradle of reposing age;
> With lenient arts extend a mother's breath,
> Make languor smile, and smooth the bed of death;
> Explore the thought, explain the asking eye,
> And keep awhile one parent from the sky."

And now I commend all this precious and splendid young womanhood before me to-day to the God "who setteth the solitary in families."

CLANDESTINE MARRIAGE.

> "Stolen waters are sweet, and bread eaten in secret is pleasant. But he knoweth not that the dead are there."—PROVERBS 9:17, 18.

The Garden of Eden was a great orchard of fruit-bearing trees, bushels and bushels of round, ripe, glorious fruit; but the horticulturist and his wife having it in charge hankered for one special tree, simply because it was forbidden, starting a bad streak in human nature, so that children will now sometimes do something simply because they are forbidden to do it. This

KINK IN THE HUMAN RACE

is not easily unsnarled. Tell a company that they may look into any twenty rooms of a large house except one, and their chief desire is to see that one, though all the others were picture-galleries and that a garret. If there were in a region of mineral springs twenty fountains, but the proprietor had fenced in one well against the public, the one fenced in would be the chief temptation to the visitors, and they would rather taste of that than of the other nineteen. Solomon recognized this principle in the text, and also the disaster that follows forbidden conduct, when he said: "Stolen waters are sweet, and bread eaten in secret is pleasant. But he knoweth not that the dead are there."

In this course of sermons on "The Wedding Ring," I this morning aim a point-blank shot at "Clandestine Marriages and Escapades."

Yonder comes up through the narrows of New York harbor a ship having all the evidence of tempestuous passage: salt water-mark reaching to the top of the smoke-stack; mainmast, foremast, mizzenmast twisted off; bulwarks knocked in; lifeboats off the davit; jib-sheets and lee-bowlines missing; captain's bridge demolished; main shaft broken; all the pumps working to keep from sinking before they can get to wharfage. That ship is the institution of Christian marriage, launched by the Lord grandly from the banks of the Euphrates, and floating out on the seas for the admiration and happiness of all nations. But free-loveism struck it from one side, and Mormonism struck it from another side, and hurricanes of libertinism have struck it on all sides, until the old ship needs repairs in every plank, and beam, and sail, and bolt, and clamp, and transom, and stanchion. In other words, the notions of modern society must be reconstructed on the subject of the marriage institution. And when we have got it back somewhere near what it was when God built it in Paradise, the earth will be far on toward resumption of Paradisaical conditions.

DEPLORABLE LAXITY.

Do you ask what is the need of a course of sermons on this subject? The man or woman who asks this question is either ignorant or guilty. In New England, which has been considered by many the most moral part of the United States, there are two thousand divorces per year. And in Massachusetts, the headquarters of steady habits, there is one divorce to every fourteen marriages. The State of Maine, considered by many almost frigid in proprieties, has in one year four hundred and seventy-eight divorces. In Vermont *swapping wives* is not a rare transaction. In Connecticut there are women who boast that they have four or five times been divorced. Moreover, our boasted Protestantism is, on this subject, more lax than Roman Catholicism. Roman Catholicism admits of no divorce except for the reason that Christ admitted as a lawful reason. But Protestantism is admitting anything and everything, and the larger the proportion of Protestants in any part of the country, the larger the ratio of divorce. Do you not then think that Protestantism needs some toning up on this subject?

GROWING POPULARITY.

Aye, when you realize that the sacred and divine institution is being caricatured and defamed by clandestine marriages and escapades all over the land, does there not seem a call for such discussion? Hardly a morning or evening paper comes into your possession without reporting them, and there are fifty of these occurrences where one is reported, because it is the interest of all parties to hush them up. The victims are, all hours of the night, climbing down ladders or crossing over from State to State, that they may reach laws of greater laxity, holding reception six months after marriage to let the public know for the first time that a half year before they were united in wedlock. Ministers of religion, and justices of the peace, and mayors of cities, willingly joining in marriage runaways from other States and neighborhoods; the coach-box and the back seat of the princely landau in flirtation; telegrams flashing across the country for the arrest of absconded school misses, who started off with arm full of books, and taking rail trains to meet their affianced—in the snow-drifts of the great storm that has recently passed over the country some of them, I read, have perished—thousands of people in a marriage whose banns have never been published; precipitated conjugality; bigamy triumphant; marriage a joke; society blotched all over with a putrefaction on this subject which no one but the Almighty God can arrest.

We admit that clandestinity and escapade are sometimes authorized and made right by parental tyranny or domestic serfdom. There have been exceptional cases where parents have had a monomania in regard to their sons and daughters, demanding their celibacy or forbidding relations every way right. Through absurd family ambition parents have sometimes demanded qualifications and equipment of fortune unreasonable to expect or simply impossible. Children are not expected to marry to please their parents, but to please themselves. Given good morals, means of a livelihood, appropriate age and quality of social position, and no parent has a right to prohibit a union that seems deliberate and a matter of the heart. Rev. Philip Henry, eminent for piety and good sense, used to say to his children: "Please God and please yourselves, and you shall never displease me."

A MATRIMONIAL TRAGEDY.

During our Civil War a marriage was about to be celebrated at Charleston, S.C., between Lieutenant de Rochelle and Miss Anna, the daughter of ex-Governor Pickens. As the ceremony was about to be solemnized a shell broke through the roof and wounded nine of the guests, and the bride fell dying, and, wrapped in her white wedding robe, her betrothed kneeling at her side, in two hours she expired. And there has been many as bright a union of hearts as that proposed that the bombshell of outrageous parental indignation has wounded and scattered and slain.

If the hand offered in marriage be blotched of intemperance; if the life of the marital candidate has been debauched; if he has no visible means of support, and poverty and abandonment seem only a little way ahead; if the twain seem entirely unmatched in disposition, protest and forbid, and re-enforce your opinion by that of others, and put all lawful obstacles in the way; but do not join that company of parents who have ruined their children by a plutocracy of domestic crankiness which has caused more than one elopement. I know of a few cases where marriage has been under the red-hot anathema of parents and all the neighbors, but God approved, and the homes established have been beautiful and positively Edenic.

But while we have admitted there are real cases of justifiable rebellion, in ninety-nine cases out of a hundred—yea, in nine hundred and ninety-nine cases out of a thousand, these unlicensed departures and decampments by moonlight are ruin, temporal and eternal. It is safer for a woman to jump off the docks of the East River and depend on being able to swim to the other shore, or get picked up by a ferry-boat. The possibilities are that she may be rescued, but the probability is that she will not. Read the story of the escapades in the newspapers for the last ten years, and find me a half dozen that do not mean poverty, disgrace, abandonment, police court, divorce, death, and hell. "Stolen waters are sweet, and bread eaten in secret is pleasant. But he knoweth not that the dead are there." Satan presides over the escapade. He introduces the two parties to each other. He gets them to pledge their troth. He appoints where they shall meet. He shows them where they can find officiating minister or squire. He points out to them the ticket office for the rail train. He puts them aboard, and when they are going at forty miles the hour he jumps off and leaves them in the lurch; for, while Satan has a genius in getting people into trouble, he has no genius for getting people out. He induced Jonah to take ship for Tarshish when God told him to go to Nineveh, but provided for the recreant prophet no better landing-place than the middle of the Mediterranean Sea.

THE DIME NOVEL.

The modern novel is responsible for many of these abscondings. Do you think that young women would sit up half a night reading novels in which the hero and heroine get acquainted in the usual way, and carry on their increased friendliness until, with the consent of parents, the day of marriage is appointed, and amid the surrounding group of kindred the vows are taken? Oh, no! There must be flight, and pursuit, and narrow escape, and drawn dagger, all ending in sunshine, and parental forgiveness, and bliss unalloyed and gorgeous. In many of the cases of escapade the idea was implanted in the hot brain of the woman by a cheap novel, ten cents' worth of unadulterated perdition.

THE SCHEME OF BAD MEN.

These evasions of the ordinary modes of marriage are to be deplored for the reason that nearly all of them are proposed by bad men. If the man behave well he has a character to which he can refer, and he can say: "If you want to inquire about me there is a list of names of people in the town or neighborhood where I live." No; the heroes of escapades are nearly all either bigamists, or libertines, or drunkards, or defrauders, or first-class scoundrels of some sort. They have no character to lose. They may be dressed in the height of fashion, may be cologned, and pomatumed, and padded, and diamond-ringed, and flamboyant-cravatted, until they bewitch the eye and intoxicate the olfactories; but they are double-distilled extracts of villainy, moral dirt and blasphemy. Beware of them. "Stolen waters are sweet, and bread eaten in secret is pleasant. But he knoweth not that the dead are there."

SOCIAL DEGRADATION.

Fugitive marriage is to be deplored because it almost always implies woman's descent from a higher social plane to a lower. If the man was not of a higher plane, or the marriage on an equality, there would be no objections, and hence no inducement to clandestinity. In almost all cases it means the lowering of womanhood. Observe this law: a man marrying a woman beneath him in society may raise her to any eminence that he himself may reach; but if a woman marry a man beneath her in society she always goes down to his level. That is a law inexorable, and there are no exceptions. Is any woman so high up that she can afford to plot for her own debasement? There is not a State in the American Union that has not for the last twenty years furnished an instance of the sudden departure of some intelligent woman from an affluent home to spend her life with some one who can make five dollars a day, provided he keeps very busy. Well, many a man has lived on five dollars a day and been happy, but he undertakes a big contract when with five dollars a day he attempts to support some one who has lived in a home that cost twenty thousand per annum. This has been about the history of most of such conjunctions of simplicity and extravagance, the marriage of

OX AND EAGLE.

The first year they get on tolerably well, for it is odd and romantic, and assisted by applause of people who admire outlawry. The second year the couple settle down into complete dislike of each other. The third year they separate and seek for divorce, or, as is more probable, the man becomes a drunkard, and the woman a blackened waif of the street. "Stolen waters are sweet, and bread eaten in secret is pleasant. But he knoweth not that the dead are there."

These truant marriages are also to be deplored because in most instances they are executed in defiance of parental wisdom and kindness. Most parents are anxious for the best welfare of a child. If they make vehement and determined opposition, it is largely because it is a match unfit to be made, and they can see for their daughter nothing but wretchedness in that direction. They have keener and wiser appreciation, for instance, of the certain domestic demolition that comes from alcoholism in a young man. They realize what an idiot a woman is who marries a man who has not brains or industry enough to earn a livelihood for a family. No bureau of statistics can tell us the number of women who, after marriage, have to support themselves and their husbands. If the husband becomes invalid, it is a beautiful thing to see a wife uncomplainingly, by needle, or pen, or yard-stick, or washing-machine, support the home. But these great, lazy masculine louts that stand around with hands in their pockets, allowing the wife with her weak arm to fight the battle of bread, need to be regurgitated from society.

REVERSED RELATIONS.

There are innumerable instances in these cities where the wife pays the rent, and meets all the family expenses, and furnishes the tobacco and the beer for the lord of the household. No wonder parents put on all the brakes to stop such a train of disaster. They have too often seen the gold ring put on the finger at the altar turning out to be the iron link of a chain of domestic servitude. What a farce it is for a man who cannot support himself, and not worth a cent in the world, to take a ring which he purchased by money stolen from his grandmother's cupboard, and put it on the finger of the bride, saying: "With this ring I thee wed, and with all my worldly goods I thee endow."

It is amazing to see how some women will marry men knowing nothing about them. No merchant would sell a hundred dollars' worth of goods on credit without knowing whether the customer was worthy of being trusted.

No man or woman would buy a house with encumbrances of mortgages, and liens, and judgments against it uncancelled; and yet there is not an hour of the day or night for the last ten years there have not been women by hasty marriage entrusting their earthly happiness to men about whose honesty they know nothing, or who are encumbered with liens, and judgments, and first mortgages, and second mortgages, and third mortgages of evil habits. No wonder that in such circumstances parents in conjugating the verb in question pass from the subjunctive mood to the indicative, and from the indicative to the imperative. In nearly all the cases of escapade that you will hear of the rest of your lives there will be a headlong leap over the barriers of parental common sense and forethought. "Stolen waters are sweet, and bread eaten in secret is pleasant. But he knoweth not that the dead are there."

INVOLVES DECEPTION.

We also deplore these fraudulent espousals and this sneaking exchange of single life for married life because it is deception, and that is a corroding and damning vice. You must deceive your kindred, you must deceive society, you must deceive all but God, and Him you cannot deceive. Deception does not injure others so much as it injures ourselves. Marriage is too important a crisis in one's life to be decided by sleight of hand, or a sort of jugglery which says: "Presto, change! Now you see her, and now you don't."

Better to wait for years for circumstances to improve. Time may remove all obstacles. The candidate for marital preferences may change his habits, or get into some trade or business that will support a home, or the inexorable father and mother may be promoted to celestial citizenship. At the right time have the day appointed. Stand at the end of the best room in the house with joined hands, and minister of religion before you to challenge the world that "if they know of any reason why these two persons shall not be united, they state it now or forever hold their peace," and then start out with the good wishes of all the neighbors and the halo of the Divine sanction. When you can go out of harbor at noon with all flags flying, do not try to run a blockade at midnight.

In view of all this, I charge you to break up clandestine correspondence if you are engaged in it, and have no more clandestine meetings, either at the ferry, or on the street, or at the house of mutual friends, or at the corner of the woods. Do not have letters come for you to the post-office under assumed address. Have no correspondence that makes you uneasy lest some one by mistake open your letters. Do not employ terms of endearment at the beginning and close of letters unless you have a right to use them. That young lady is on the edge of danger who dares not allow her mother to see her letters.

CONFIDE IN PARENTS.

If you have sensible parents take them into your confidence in all the affairs of the heart. They will give you more good advice in one hour than you can get from all the world beside in five years. They have toiled for you so long, and prayed for you so much, they have your best interests at heart. At the same time let parents review their opposition to a proposed marital alliance, and see if their opposition is founded on a genuine wish for the child's welfare, or on some whim, or notion, or prejudice, or selfishness, fighting a natural law and trying to make Niagara run up stream. William Pitt, the Prime Minister of England in the reign of George III., was always saying wise things. One day Sir Walter Farquhar called on him in great perturbation. Mr. Pitt inquired what was the matter, and Sir Walter told him that his daughter was about to be married to one not worthy of her rank. Mr. Pitt said: "Is the young man of respectable family?" "Yes." "Is he respectable in himself?" "Yes." "Has he an estimable character?" "Yes." "Why, then, my dear Sir Walter, make no opposition." The advice was taken, and a happy married life ensued. Let ministers and officers of the law decline officiating at clandestine marriages. When they are asked to date a marriage certificate back, as we all are asked, let them peremptorily decline to say that the ceremony was in November instead of January, or decline to leave the date blank, lest others fill out the record erroneously. Let a law be passed in all our States, as it has already been in some of the States, making a license from officers of the law necessary before we can unite couples, and then make it necessary to publish beforehand in the newspapers, as it used to be published in the New England churches, so that if there be lawful objection it may be presented, not swinging the buoy on the rocks after the ship has struck and gone to pieces.

And here it might be well for me to take all the romance out of an escapade by quoting a dozen lines of Robert Pollock, the great Scotch poet, where he describes the crazed victim of one of these escapades:

"... Yet had she many days
Of sorrow in the world, but never wept.
She lived on alms, and carried in her hand
Some withered stalks she gathered in the spring.
When any asked the cause she smiled, and said
They were her sisters, and would come and watch
Her grave when she was dead. She never spoke
Of her deceiver, father, mother, home,
Or child, or heaven, or hell, or God; but still
In lonely places walked, and ever gazed
Upon the withered stalks, and talked to them;
Till, wasted to the shadow of her youth,
With woe too wide to see beyond, she died."

UNDER THE LIGHT.

But now I turn on this subject an intenser light. We have fifteen hundred lights in this church, and when by electric touch they are kindled in the evening service it is almost startling. But this whole subject of "Clandestine Marriages and Escapades" I put under a more intense light than that. The headlight of a locomotive is terrible if you stand near enough to catch the full glare of it. As it sweeps around the "Horseshoe Curve" of the Alleghanies or along the edges of the Sierra Nevadas, how far ahead, and how deep down, and how high up it flashes, and there is instantaneous revelation of mountain peak and wild beasts hieing themselves to their caverns and cascades a thousand feet tall, or clinging in white terror to the precipices! But more intense, more far-reaching, more sudden, swifter and more tremendous is the headlight of an advancing Judgment Day, under which all the most hidden affairs of life shall come to discovery and arraignment. I quote an overwhelming passage of Scripture, in which I put the whole emphasis on the word "secret." "God shall bring every work into judgment, with every secret thing, whether it be good or evil."

What a time that will be in which the cover shall be lifted from every home and from every heart. The iniquity may have been so sly that it escaped all human detection, but it will be as well known on that day as the crimes of Sodom and Gomorrah, unless for Christ's sake it has been forgiven. All the fingers of universal condemnation will be pointed at it. The archangel of wrath will stand there with uplifted thunderbolt ready to strike it. The squeamishness and prudery of earthly society, which hardly allowed some sins to be mentioned on earth, are past, and the man who was unclean and the woman who was impure will, under a light brighter than a thousand noonday suns, stand with the whole story written on scalp, and forehead, and cheek, and hands, and feet; the whole resurrection body aflame and dripping with fiery disclosures, ten thousand sepulchral and celestial and infernal voices crying, "Unclean! Unclean! Unclean!"

All marital intrigues and all secret iniquities will be published, as though all the trumpets spoke them, and all the lightnings capitalized them, and all the earthquakes rumbled them. Oh, man, recreant to thy marriage vow! Oh, woman, in sinful collusion! What, then, will become of thy poor soul? The tumbling Alps, and Pyrenees, and Mount Washingtons cannot hide thee from the consequences of thy secret sins. Better repent of them now, so that they cannot be brought against thee. For the chief of sinners there is pardon, if you ask it in time. But I leave you to guess what chance there will be for those who on earth lived in clandestine relations, when on that day the very Christ who had such high appreciation of the marriage relation that He compared it to His own relation with the Church, shall appear at the door of the great hall of the Last Assize, and all the multitudes of earth, and hell, and heaven shall rise up and cry out from the three galleries: "Behold, the bridegroom cometh!"

DUTIES OF HUSBANDS TO WIVES.ToC

"And Isaac went out to meditate in the field at eventide: and he lifted up his eyes, and saw, and, behold, the camels were coming."—GENESIS 24:63.

A bridal pageant on the back of dromedaries! The camel is called the ship of the desert. Its swinging motion in the distance is suggestive of a vessel rising and falling with the billows. Though awkward, how imposing these creatures as they move along, whether in ancient or modern times, sometimes carrying four hundred or four thousand travelers from Bagdad to Aleppo, or from Bassora to Damascus! In my text comes a caravan. We notice the noiseless step of the broad foot, the velocity of motion, the gay caparison of saddle, and girth, and awning, sheltering the riders from the sun, and the hilarity of the mounted passengers, and we cry out: "Who are they?" Well, Isaac has been praying for a wife, and it is time he had one, for he is forty years of age; and his servant, directed by the Lord, has made a selection of Rebekah; and, with her companions and maidens, she is on her way to her new home, carrying with her the blessing of all her friends.

THE NUPTIAL MEETING.

Isaac is in the fields, meditating upon his proposed passage from celibacy to monogamy. And he sees a speck against the sky, then groups of people, and after a while he finds that the grandest earthly blessing that ever comes to a man is approaching with this gay caravan.

In this my discourse on "The Wedding Ring," having spoken of the choice of a lifetime companion, I take it for granted, O man, that your marriage was divinely arranged, and that the camels have arrived from the right direction and at the right time, bringing the one that was intended for your consort—a Rebekah and not a Jezebel. I proceed to discuss as to how you ought to treat your wife, and my ambition is to tell you more plain truth than you ever heard in any three-quarters of an hour in all your life.

THE RESPONSIBILITY UNDERTAKEN.

First of all, I charge you realize your responsibility in having taken her from the custody and care and homestead in which she was once sheltered. What courage you must have had, and what confidence in yourself, to say to her practically: "I will be to you more than your father and mother, more than all the friends you ever had or ever can have! Give up everything and take me. I feel competent to see you through life in safety. You are an immortal being, but I am competent to defend you and make you happy. However bright and comfortable a home you have now, and though in one of the rooms is the arm-chair in which you rocked, and in the garret is the cradle in which you were hushed and the trundle-bed in which you slept, and in the sitting-room are the father and mother who have got wrinkle-faced, and stoop-shouldered, and dim-eyesighted in taking care of you, yet you will do better to come with me." I am amazed that any of us ever had the sublimity of impudence to ask such a transfer from a home assured to a home conjectured and unbuilt.

A RISKY VOYAGE.

You would think me a very daring and hazardous adventurer if I should go down to one of the piers on the North River, and at a time when there was a great lack of ship captains, and I should, with no knowledge of navigation, propose to take a steamer across to Glasgow or Havre, and say: "All aboard! Haul in the planks and swing out," and, passing out into the sea, plunge through darkness and storm. If I succeeded in getting charge of a ship, it would be one that would never be heard of again. But that is the boldness of every man that proffers marriage. He says: "I will navigate you through the storms, the cyclones, the fogs of a lifetime. I will run clear of rocks and icebergs. I have no experience and I have no seaport, but all aboard for the voyage of a lifetime! I admit that there have been ten thousand shipwrecks on this very route, but don't hesitate! Tut! Tut! There now! Don't cry! Brides must not cry at the wedding."

THE WIFE'S TEMERITY.

In response to this the woman, by her action, practically says: "I have but one life to live, and I entrust it all to you. My arm is weak, but I will depend on the strength of yours. I don't know much of the world, but I rely on your wisdom. I put my body, my mind, my soul, my time, my eternity, in your keeping. I make no reserve. Even my name I resign and take yours, though mine is a name that suggests all that was honorable in my father, and all that was good in my mother, and all that was pleasant in my brothers and sisters. I start with you on a journey which shall not part except at the edge of your grave or mine. Ruth, the Moabitess, made no more thorough self-abnegation than I make, when I take her tremendous words, the pathos of which many centuries have not cooled:

Entreat me not to leave thee, or to return from following after thee; for whither thou goest, I will go, and where thou lodgest, I will lodge. Thy people shall be my people, and thy God my God. Where thou diest will I die, and there will I be buried. The Lord do so to me and more also, if aught but death part thee and me.' Side by side in life. Side by side in the burying-ground. Side by side in heaven. Before God and man, and with my immortal soul in the oath, I swear eternal fidelity."

ENTITLED TO ADMIRATION.

Now, my brother, how ought you to treat her? Unless you are an ingrate infinite you will treat her well. You will treat her better than any one in the universe except your God. Her name will have in it more music than in all that Chopin, or Bach, or Rheinberger composed. Her eyes, swollen with three weeks of night watching over a child with scarlet fever, will be to you beautiful as a May morning. After the last rose petal has dropped out of her cheek, after the last feather of the raven's wing has fallen from her hair, after across her forehead, and under her eyes, and across her face there are as many wrinkles as there are graves over which she has wept, you will be able truthfully to say, in the words of Solomon's song: "Behold, thou art fair, my love! Behold, thou art fair!" And perhaps she may respond appropriately in the words that no one but the matchless Robert Burns could ever have found pen or ink, or heart or brain to write:

> "John Anderson, my jo, John,
>   We clamb the hill thegither;
> And mony a canty day, John,
>   We've had wi' ane anither.
> Now we maun totter down, John,
>   But hand in hand we'll go;
> And sleep thegither at the foot,
>   John Anderson, my jo."

If any one assail her good name, you will have hard work to control your temper, and if you should strike him down the sin will not be unpardonable. By as complete a surrender as the universe ever saw—except that of the Son of God for your salvation and mine—she has a first mortgage on your body, mind and soul, and the mortgage is foreclosed; and you do not more thoroughly own your two eyes or your two hands than she owns you. The longer the journey Rebekah makes and the greater the risks of her expedition on the back of the camels, the more thoroughly is Isaac bound to be kind, and indulgent, and worthy.

LOVERS' PROMISES BINDING.

Now, be honest and pay your debts. You promised to make her happy. Are you making her happy? You are an honest man in other things, and feel the importance of keeping a contract. If you have induced her into a conjugal partnership under certain pledges of kindness and valuable attention, and then have failed to fulfill your word, you deserve to have a suit brought against you for getting goods under false pretences, and then you ought to be mulcted in a large amount of damages. Review now all the fine, beautiful, complimentary, gracious and glorious things you promised her before marriage and reflect whether you have kept your faith. Do you say, "Oh, that was all sentimentalism, and romance, and a joke," and that "they all talk that way!" Well, let that plan be tried on yourself! Suppose I am interested in Western lands, and I fill your mind with roseate speculation, and I tell you that a city is already laid out on the farm that I propose to sell you, and that a new railroad will run close by, and have a depot for easy transportation of the crops, and that eight or ten capitalists are going to put up fine residences close by, and that the climate is delicious, and that the ground, high up, gives no room for malaria, and that every dollar planted will grow up into a bush bearing ten or twenty dollars, and my speech glows with enthusiasm until you rush off with me to an attorney to have the deed drawn, and the money paid down, and the bargain completed. You can hardly sleep nights because of the El Dorado, the Elysium, upon which you are soon to enter.

A WESTERN EDEN.

You give up your home at the East, you bid good-bye to your old neighbors, and take the train, and after many days' journey you arrive at a quiet depot, from which you take a wagon thirty miles through the wilderness, and reach your new place. You see a man seated on a wet log, in a swamp, and shaking with the fifteenth attack of chills and fever, and ask him who he is. He says: "I am a real estate agent, having in charge the property around here." You ask him where the new depot is. He tells you that it has not yet been built, but no doubt will be if the company get their bill for the track through the next legislature. You ask him where the new city is laid out. He says, with chattering teeth: "If you will wait till this chill is off, I will show it to you on the map I have in my pocket." You ask him where the capitalists are going to build their fine houses, and he says: "Somewhere along those lowlands out there by those woods, when the water has been drained off." That night you sleep in the hut of the real estate agent, and though you pray for everybody else, you do not pray for me. Being more fortunate than many men who go out in such circumstances, you have money enough to get back, and you come to me, and out of breath in your indignation, you say: "You have swindled me out of everything. What do you mean in deceiving me about that Western property?" "Oh," I reply, "that was all right; that was sentimentalism, and romance, and a joke. That's the way they all talk!"

But more excusable would I be in such deception than you, O man, who by glow of words and personal magnetism induced a womanly soul into surroundings which you have taken no care to make attractive, so that she exchanged her father's house for the dismal swamp of married experience—treeless, flowerless, shelterless, comfortless and godless. I would not be half so much to blame in cheating you out of a farm as you in cheating a woman out of the happiness of a lifetime.

LOVERS' ATTENTIONS.

My brother, do not get mad at what I say, but honestly compare the promises you made, and see whether you have kept them. Some of you spent every evening of the week with your betrothed before marriage, and since then you spent every evening away, except you have influenza or some sickness on account of which the doctor says you must not go out. You used to fill your conversation with interjections of adulation, and now you think it sounds silly to praise the one who ought to be more attractive to you as the years go by, and life grows in severity of struggle and becomes more sacred by the baptism of tears—tears over losses, tears over graves. Compare the way some of you used to come in the house in the evening, when you were attempting the capture of her affections, and the way some of you come into the house in the evening now.

DON'T BE PREOCCUPIED.

Then what politeness, what distillation of smiles, what graciousness, sweet as the peach orchard in blossom week! Now, some of you come in and put your hat on the rack and scowl, and say: "Lost money to-day!" and you sit down at the table and criticise the way the food is cooked. You shove back before the others are done eating, and snatch up the evening paper and read, oblivious of what has been going on in that home all day. The children are in awe before the domestic autocrat. Bubbling over with fun, yet they must be quiet; with healthful curiosity, yet they must ask no questions. The wife has had enough annoyances in the nursery, and parlor, and kitchen to fill her nerves with nettles and spikes. As you have provided the money for food and wardrobe, you feel you have done all required of you. Toward the good cheer, and the intelligent improvement, and the moral entertainment of that home, which at the longest can last but a few years, you are doing nothing. You seem to have no realization of the fact that soon these children will be grown up or in their sepulchres, and will be far removed from your influence, and that the wife will soon end her earthly mission, and that house will be occupied by others, and you yourself will be gone.

Gentlemen, fulfill your contracts. Christian marriage is an affectional bargain. In heathen lands a man wins his wife by achievements. In some countries wives are bought by the payment of so many dollars, as so many cattle or sheep. In one country the man gets on a horse and rides down where a group of women are standing, and seizes one of them by the hair, and lifts her, struggling and resisting, on his horse, and if her brothers and friends do not overtake her before she gets to the jungle, she is his lawful wife. In another land the masculine candidate for marriage is beaten by the club of the one whom he would make his bride. If he cries out under the pounding, he is rejected. If he receives the blows uncomplainingly, she is his by right. Endurance, and bravery, and skill decide the marriage in barbarous lands, but Christian marriage is a voluntary bargain, in which you promise protection, support, companionship and love.

THE TERMS OF THE CONTRACT.

Business men have in their fire-proof safes a file of papers containing their contracts, and sometimes they take them out and read them over to see what the party of the first part and the party of the second part really bound themselves to do. Different ministers of religion have their own peculiar forms of marriage ceremony; but if you have forgotten what you promised at the altar of wedlock, you had better buy or borrow an Episcopal Church-

Service, which contains the substance of all intelligent marriage ceremonies, when it says: "I take thee to be my wedded wife, to have and to hold from this day forward, for better or for worse, for richer or for poorer, in sickness and in health, to love and to cherish till death us do part, according to God's holy ordinance, and thereto I pledge thee my troth." Would it not be a good idea to have that printed in tract form and widely distributed?

NEVER FLIRT.

The fact is, that many men are more kind to everybody else's wives than to their own wives. They will let the wife carry a heavy coal scuttle upstairs, and will at one bound clear the width of a parlor to pick up some other lady's pocket-handkerchief. There is an evil which I have seen under the sun, and it is common among men—namely, husbands in flirtation. The attention they ought to put upon their own wives they bestow upon others. They smile on them coyly and askance, and with a manner that seems to say: "I wish I was free from that old drudge at home. What an improvement you would be on my present surroundings!" And bouquets are sent, and accidental meetings take place, and late at night the man comes to his prosaic home, whistling and hilarious, and wonders that the wife is jealous. There are thousands of men who, while not positively immoral, need radical correction of their habits in this direction. It is meanness immeasurable for a man by his behavior to seem to say to his wife: "You can't help yourself, and I will go where I please, and admire whom I please, and I defy your criticism."

Why did you not have that put in the bond, O domestic Shylock? Why did you not have it understood before you were pronounced husband and wife that she should have only a part of the dividend of your affections; that when, as time rolled on and the cares of life had erased some of the bright lines from her face, and given unwieldiness to her form, you would have the reserved right to pay obeisance to cheeks more rubicund, and figure lither and more agile, and as you demanded the last pound of patience and endurance on her part you could, with the emphasis of an Edwin Forrest or a Macready, have tapped the eccentric marriage document and have said: "It's in the bond!" If this modern Rebekah had understood beforehand where she was alighting she would have ordered the camel drivers to turn the caravan backward toward Padan-aram. Flirtation has its origin either in dishonesty or licentiousness. The married man who indulges in it is either a fraud or a rake. However high up in society such a one may be, and however sought after, I would not give a three-cent piece, though it had been three times clipped, for the virtue of the masculine flirt.

TONE UP.

The most worthy thing for the thousands of married men to do is to go home and apologize for past neglects and brighten up their old love. Take up the family Bible and read the record of the marriage day. Open the drawer of relics in the box inside the drawer containing the trinkets of your dead child. Take up the pack of yellow-colored letters that were written before you became one. Rehearse the scenes of joy and sorrow in which you have mingled. Put all these things as fuel on the altar, and by a coal of sacred fire rekindle the extinguished light. It was a blast from hell that blew it out, and a gale from heaven will fan it into a blaze.

Ye who have broken marriage vows, speak out! take your wife into all your plans, your successes, your defeats, your ambitions. Tell her everything. Walk arm in arm with her into places of amusement, and on the piazza of summer watering places, and up the rugged way of life, and down through dark ravine, and when one trembles on the way let the other be re-enforcement. In no case pass yourself off as a single man, practicing gallantries. Do not, after you are fifty years of age, in ladies' society, try to look young-mannish.

RESPECT HER PIETY.

Interfere not with your wife's religious nature. Put her not in that awful dilemma in which so many Christian wives are placed by their husbands, who ask them to go to places or do things which compel them to decide between loyalty to God and loyalty to the husband. Rather than ask her to compromise her Christian character encourage her to be more and more a Christian, for there will be times in your life when you will want the help of all her Christian resources; and certainly, when you remember how much influence your mother had over you, you do not want the mother of your children to set a less gracious example. It pleases me greatly to hear the unconverted and worldly husband say about his wife, with no idea that it will get to her ears: "There is the most godly woman alive. Her goodness is a perpetual rebuke to my waywardness. Nothing on earth could ever induce her to do a wrong thing. I hope the children will take after her instead of after me. If there is any heaven at all I am sure she will go there."

THE PRIEST OF THE HOUSEHOLD.

Ay, my brother, do you not think it would be a wise and a safe thing for you to join her on the road to heaven? You think you have a happy home now, but what a home you would have if you both were religious! What a new sacredness it would give to your marital relation, and what a new light it would throw on the forehead of your children! In sickness, what a comfort! In reverses of fortune, what a wealth! In death, what a triumph! God meant you to be the high priest of your household. Go home to-day and take the Bible on your lap, and gather all your family yet living around you, and those not living will hear of it in a flash, and as ministering spirits will hover—father and mother and children gone, and all your celestial kindred. Then kneel down, and if you can't think of a prayer to offer I will give you a prayer—namely: "Lord God, I surrender to Thee myself and my beloved wife, and these dear children. For Christ's sake forgive all the past and help us for all the future. We have lived together here, may we live together forever. Amen and amen." Dear me, what a stir it would make among your best friends on earth and in heaven.

A HUSBAND IMPRISONED.

Joseph the Second, the Emperor, was so kind and so philanthropic that he excited the unbounded love of most of his subjects. He abolished serfdom, established toleration and lived in the happiness of his people. One day while on his way to Ostend to declare it a free port, and while at the head of a great procession, he saw a woman at the door of her cottage in dejection. The Emperor dismounted and asked the cause of her grief. She said that her husband had gone to Ostend to see the Emperor, and had declined to take her with him; for, as he was an alien, he could not understand her loyal enthusiasm, and that it was the one great desire of her life to see the ruler for whose kindness and goodness and greatness she had an unspeakable admiration; and her disappointment in not being able to go and see him was simply unbearable.

The Emperor Joseph took from his pocket a box decorated with diamonds surrounding a picture of himself and presented it to her, and when the picture revealed to whom she was talking she knelt in reverence and clapped her hands in gladness before him. The Emperor took the name of her husband and the probable place where he might be found at Ostend, and had him imprisoned for the three days of the Emperor's visit, so that the husband returning home found that the wife had seen the Emperor while he had not seen him.

In many families of this earth the wife, through the converting grace of God, has seen the "King in His beauty," and He has conferred upon her the pearl of great price, while the husband is an "alien from the covenant of promise, without God and without hope in the world," and imprisoned in worldliness and sin. Oh, that they might arm in arm go this day and see Him, who is not only greater and lovelier than any Joseph of earthly dominion, but "high over all, in earth, and air, and sky!" His touch is life. His voice is music. His smile is heaven.

DUTIES OF WIVES TO HUSBANDS.ToC

> "The name of his wife was Abigail; and she was a woman of good understanding and of a beautiful countenance."—1 SAMUEL 25:3.

The ground in Carmel is white, not with fallen snow, but the wool from the backs of three thousand sheep, for they are being sheared. And I hear the grinding of the iron blades together, and the bleating of the flocks, held between the knees of the shearers, while the clipping goes on, and the rustic laughter of the workmen. Nabal and his wife Abigail preside over this homestead. David, the warrior, sends a delegation to apply for aid at this prosperous time of sheep-shearing, and Nabal peremptorily declines his request. Revenge is the cry. Yonder over the rocks come David and four hundred angry men with one stroke to demolish Nabal and his sheepfolds and vineyards. The regiment marches in double quick, and the stones of the mountain loosen and roll down, as the soldiers strike them with their swift feet, and the cry of the commander is "Forward! Forward!"

A FAIR PROPITIATOR.

Abigail, to save her husband and his property, hastens to the foot of the hill. She is armed, not with sword or spear, but with her own beauty and self-sacrifice, and when David sees her kneeling at the base of the craig, he cries: "Halt! Halt!" and the caverns echo it: "Halt! Halt!" Abigail is the conqueress! One woman in the right mightier than four hundred men in the wrong! A hurricane stopped at the sight of a water-lily! A dewdrop dashed back Niagara! By her prowess and tact she has saved her husband, and saved her home, and put before all ages an illustrious specimen of what a wife can do if she be godly, and prudent, and self-sacrificing, and vigilant, and devoted to the interests of her husband, and attractive.

As, Sabbath before last, I took the responsibility of telling husbands how they ought to treat their wives—and, though I noticed that some of the men squirmed a little in their pew, they endured it well—I now take the responsibility of telling how wives ought to treat their husbands. I hope your domestic alliance was so happily formed that while married life may have revealed in him some frailties that you did not suspect, it has also displayed excellencies that more than overbalanced them. I suppose that if I could look into the heart of a hundred wives here present and ask them where is the kindest and best man they know of, and they dared speak out, ninety-nine out of a hundred of them would say: "At the other end of this pew."

ABIGAIL'S BAD BARGAIN.

I hope, my sister, you have married a man as Christian and as well balanced as that. But even if you were worsted in conjugal bargain, you cannot be worse off than this Abigail in my text. Her husband was cross and ungrateful, an inebriate, for on the very evening after her heroic achievement at the foot of the hill, where she captured a whole regiment with her genial and strategic behaviour, she returned home and found her husband so drunk that she could not tell him the story, but had to postpone it until the next day. So, my sister, I do not want you to keep saying within yourself as I proceed: "That is the way to treat a perfect husband;" for you are to remember that no wife was ever worse swindled than this Abigail of my text. At the other end of her table sat a mean, selfish, snarling, contemptible sot, and if she could do so well for a dastard, how ought you to do with that princely and splendid man with whom you are to walk the path of life?

First, I counsel the wife to remember in what a severe and terrific battle of life her husband is engaged. Whether in professional, or commercial, or artistic, or mechanical life, your husband from morning to night is in a Solferino, if not a Sedan. It is a wonder that your husband has any nerves or patience or suavity left. To get a living in this next to the last decade of the nineteenth century is a struggle. If he come home and sit down preoccupied, you ought to excuse him. If he do not feel like going out that night for a walk or entertainment, remember he has been out all day. You say he ought to leave at his place of business his annoyances and come home cheery. But if a man has been betrayed by a business partner, or a customer has cheated him out of a large bill of goods, or a protested note has been flung on his desk, or somebody has called him a liar, and everything has gone wrong from morning till night, he must have great genius and forgetfulness if he do not bring some of the perplexity home with him. When you tell me he ought to leave it all at the store or bank or shop, you might as well tell a storm on the Atlantic to stay out there and not touch the coast or ripple the harbor.

RESPECT SELF-SACRIFICE.

Remember, he is not overworking so much for himself as he is overworking for you and the children. It is the effect of his success or defeat on the homestead that causes him the agitation. The most of men after forty-five years of age live not for themselves, but for their families. They begin to ask themselves anxiously the question: "How if I should give out, what would become of the folks at home? Would my children ever get their education? Would my wife have to go out into the world to earn bread for herself and our little ones? My eyesight troubles me; how if my eyes should fail? My head gets dizzy; how if I should drop under apoplexy?" The high pressure of business life and mechanical life and agricultural life is home pressure.

Some time ago a large London firm decided that if any of their clerks married on a salary less than £150—that is, $750 a year—he should be discharged, the supposition being that the temptation might be too great for misappropriation. The large majority of families in America live by utmost dint of economy, and to be honest and yet meet one's family expenses is the appalling question that turns the life of tens of thousands of men into martyrdom. Let the wife of the overborne and exhausted husband remember this, and do not nag him about that, and say you might as well have no husband when the fact is he is dying by inches that the home may be kept up.

BE LOVABLE.

I charge also the wife to keep herself as attractive after marriage as she was before marriage. The reason that so often a man ceases to love his wife is because the wife ceases to be lovable. In many cases what elaboration of toilet before marriage, and what recklessness of appearance after! The most disgusting thing on earth is a slatternly woman—I mean a woman who never combs her hair until she goes out, or looks like a fright until somebody calls. That a man married to one of these creatures stays at home as little as possible is no wonder. It is a wonder that such a man does not go on a whaling voyage of three years, and in a leaky ship. Costly wardrobe is not required; but, O woman! if you are not willing, by all that ingenuity of refinement can effect, to make yourself attractive to your husband, you ought not to complain if he seek in other society those pleasant surroundings which you deny him.

DO NOT COMPLAIN.

Again, I charge you never talk to others about the frailties of your husband.[1] Some people have a way, in banter, of elaborately describing to others the shortcomings or unhappy eccentricities of a husband or wife. Ah, the world will find out soon enough all the defects of your companion! No need of your advertising them! Better imitate those women who, having made mistake in affiance, always have a veil to hide imperfections and alleviations of conduct to mention. We must admit that there are rare cases where a wife cannot live longer with her husband, and his cruelties and outrages are the precursor of divorcement or separation. But until that day comes, keep the awful secret to yourself—keep it from every being in the universe except the God to whom you do well to tell your trouble. Trouble only a few years at most, and then you can go up on the other side of the grave, and say: "O Lord, I kept the marital secret! Thou knowest how well I kept it, and I thank Thee that the release has come at last. Give me some place where I can sit down and rest awhile from the horrors of an embruted earthly alliance, before I begin the full raptures of heaven." And orders will be sent out to the usher angels, saying: "Take this Abigail right up to the softest seat in the best room of the palace, and let twenty of the brightest angels wait on her for the next thousand years."

AVOID MEDDLERS.

Further, I charge you, let there be no outside interference with the conjugal relation. Neither neighbor nor confidential friend, nor brother, nor sister, nor father, nor mother, have a right to come in here. The married gossip will come around, and by the hour tell you how she manages her husband. You tell her plainly that if she will attend to the affairs of her household you will attend to yours. What damage some people do with their tongues! Nature indicates that the tongue is a dangerous thing, by the fact that it is shut in, first by a barricade of teeth, and then by the door of the lips. One insidious talker can keep a whole neighborhood badly stirred up. The Apostle Peter excoriated these busybodies in other people's matters, and St. Paul, in his letter to the Thessalonians and to Timothy, gives them a sharp dig, and the good housewife will be on the lookout for them, and never return their calls, and treat them with coldest frigidity. For this reason, better keep house as soon as possible. Some people are opposed to them, but I thank God for what are called flats in these cities. They put a separate home within the means of nearly all the population. In your married relations you do not need any advice. If you and your husband have not skill enough to get along well alone, with all the advice you can import you will get along worse. What you want for your craft on this voyage is plenty of sea-room.

BE INTELLIGENT.

I charge you, also, make yourself the intelligent companion of your husband. What with these floods of newspapers and books there is no excuse for the wife's ignorance either about the present or the past. If you have no more than a half-hour every day to yourself you may fill your mind with entertaining and useful knowledge. Let the merchant's wife read up on all mercantile questions, and the mechanic's wife on all that pertains to his style of work, and the professional man's wife on all the legal, or medical, or theological, or political discussions of the day. It is very stupid for a man, after having been amid active minds all day, to find his wife without information or opinions on anything. If the wife knows nothing about what is going on in the world, after the tea-hour has passed, and the husband has read the newspaper, he will have an engagement and must "go and see a man." In nine cases out of ten when a man does not stay at home in the evening, unless positive duty calls him away, it is because there is nothing to stay for. He would rather talk with his wife than anyone else if she could talk as well.

ADORN THE HOME.

I charge you, my sister, in every way to make your home attractive. I have not enough of practical knowledge about house adornment to know just what makes the difference, but here is an opulent house, containing all wealth of *bric-a-brac*, and of musical instrument, and of painting, and of upholstery, and yet there is in it a chill like Nova Zembla. Another home, with one-twentieth part of the outlay, and small supply of art, and cheapest piano purchasable, and yet, as you enter it, there comes upon body, mind, and soul a glow of welcome and satisfied and happy domesticity. The holy art of making the most comfort and brightness out of the means afforded, every wife should study.

At the siege of Argus, Pyrrhus was killed by the tile of a roof thrown by a woman, and Abimelech was slain by a stone that a woman threw from the tower of Thebes, and Earl Montfort was destroyed by a rock discharged at him by a woman from the walls of Toulouse. But without any weapon save that of her cold, cheerless household arrangement, any wife may slay all the attractions of a home circle. A wife and mother in prosperous circumstances and greatly admired was giving her chief time to social life. The husband spent his evenings away. The son, fifteen years of age, got the same habit, and there was a prospect that the other children, as they got old enough, would take the same turn. One day the wife aroused to the consideration that she had better save her husband and her boy. Interesting and stirring games were introduced into the house. The mother studied up interesting things to tell her children. One morning the son said:

"Father, you ought to have been home last night. We had a grand time. Such jolly games and such interesting stories!" This went on from night to night, and after a while the husband stayed in to see what was going on, and he finally got attracted, and added something of his own to the evening entertainments; and the result was that the wife and mother saved her husband and saved her boy and saved herself. Was not that an enterprise worth the attention of the greatest woman that ever lived since Abigail at the foot of the rock arrested the four hundred armed warriors?

THE TRUE SPHERE.

Do not, my sister, be dizzied and disturbed by the talk of those who think the home circle too insignificant for a woman's career, and who want to get you out on platforms and in conspicuous enterprises. There are women who have a special outside mission, and do not dare to interpret me as derisive of their important mission. But my opinion is that the woman who can reinforce her husband in the work of life and rear her children for positions of usefulness is doing more for God and the race and her own happiness than if she spoke on every great platform and headed a hundred great enterprises. My mother never made a missionary speech in her life, and at a missionary meeting I doubt whether she could have got enough courage to vote aye or no, but she raised her son John, who has been preaching the Gospel and translating religious literature in Amoy, China, for about forty years. Was not that a better thing to do?

Compare such an one with one of these dieaway, attitudinizing, frivolous, married coquettes of the modern drawing-room, her heaven an opera box on the night of Meyerbeer's "Robert le Diable," the ten commandments an inconvenience, taking arsenic to improve the complexion, and her appearance a confused result of belladonna, bleached hair, antimony and mineral acids, until one is compelled to discuss her character, and wonder whether the line between a decent and indecent life is, like the equator, an imaginary line.

A PRESSING WANT.

What the world wants now is about fifty thousand old-fashioned mothers, women who shall realize that the highest, grandest, mightiest institution on earth is the home. It is not necessary that they should have the same old-time manners of the country farm-house, or wear the old-fashioned cap and spectacles and apron that her glorified ancestry wore; but I mean the old spirit which began with the Hannahs and the Mother Lois and the Abigails of Scripture days, and was demonstrated on the homestead where some of us were reared, though the old house long ago was pulled down and its occupants scattered, never to meet until in the higher home that awaits the families of the righteous. While there are more good and faithful wives and mothers now than there ever were, society has got a wrong twist on this subject, and there are influences abroad that would make women believe that their chief sphere is outside instead of inside the home.

A DEADLY SIN.

Hence in many households, children instead of a blessing are a nuisance. It is card case *versus* child's primer, carriage *versus* cradle, social popularity *versus* domestic felicity. Hence infanticide and antenatal murder so common that all the physicians, allopathic, hydropathic, homœopathic, and eclectic are crying out in horror, and it is time that the pulpits joined with the medical profession in echoing and re-echoing the thunder of Mount Sinai, which says: "Thou shalt not kill," and the book of Revelation, which says: "All murderers shall have their place in the lake which burneth with fire and brimstone." And the man or the woman who takes life a minute old will as certainly go straight to hell as the man or woman who destroys life forty years old. And the wildest, loudest shriek of Judgment Day will be given at the overthrow of those who moved in the high and respected circles of earthly society, yet decreed by their own act, as far as they could privately effect it, the extermination of the advancing generations, abetted in the horrid crime by a lot of infernal quacks with which modern medicine is infested. When, on the Last Day, the crier of the Court shall with resounding "Oyez," "Oyez!" declare the "Oyer and Terminer" of the Universe opened, and the Judge, with gavel of thunderbolt, shall smite the nations into silence, and the trial of all the fratricides, and parricides, and matricides, and patricides, and uxoricides, and regicides, and deicides, and infanticides of the earth shall proceed, none of my hearers or readers can say that they knew not what they were doing. Mighty God! arrest the evil that is overshadowing this century.

THE HEAD OF THE HOUSEHOLD.

I charge you, my sister, that you take your husband along with you to heaven. Of course this implies that you yourself are a Christian. I must take that for granted. It cannot be possible that after what Christianity has done for woman, and after taking the infinitely responsible position you have assumed as the head of the household, that you should be in a position antagonistic to Christ. It was not a slip of the tongue when I spoke of you as being at the head of the household. We men rather pride ourselves as being at the head of the household, but it is only a pleasant delusion. To whom do the children go when they have trouble? When there is a sore finger to be bound up or one of the first teeth that needs to be removed to make way for one that is crowding it out, to whom does the child go? For whom do children cry out in the night when they get frightened at a bad dream? Aye, to whom does the husband go when he has a business trouble too great or too delicate for outside ears? We, the men, are heads of the household in name, but you, O wives! are the heads of the household in fact, and it is your business to take your husband with you into the kingdom of God, and see that house prepared for heaven.

You can do it! Of course God's almighty grace alone can convert him, but you are to be the instrument. Some wives keep their husbands out of heaven, and others garner them for it. If your religion, O wife! is simply the joke of the household, if you would rather go to the theatre than the prayer-meeting, if you can beat all the neighborhood in progressive euchre, if your husband never sees you kneel at the bedside in prayer before retiring, if the only thing that reminds the family of your church relations is that on communion-day you get home late to dinner, you will not be able to take your husband to heaven, for the simple reason that you will not get there yourself. But I suppose that your religion is genuine, and that the husband realizes that there is in your soul a divine principle, and that, though you may be naturally quicker tempered than he is and have many imperfections that distress you more than they can any one else, still you are destined for the skies when the brief scenes of this life are over. How will you take him with you? There are two oars to that boat—prayer and holy example.

But you say he belongs to a worldly club, or he does not believe a word of the Bible, or he is an inebriate and very loose in his habits? What you tell me shows that you don't understand that while you are at the one end of a prayer, the omnipotent God is at the other end, and it is simply a question whether Almightiness is strong enough and keeps His word. I have no doubt there will be great conventions in heaven, called for celebrative purposes, and when in some Celestial assemblage the saints shall be telling what brought them to God, I believe that ten thousand times ten thousand will say: "My wife."

A CONTRAST.

I put beside each other two testimonies of men concerning their wives, and let you see the contrast. An aged man was asked the reason of his salvation. With tearful emotion he said: "My wife was brought to God some years before myself. I persecuted and abused her because of her religion. She, however, returned nothing but kindness, constantly maintaining an anxiety to promote my comfort and happiness; and it was her amiable conduct when suffering ill-treatment from me that first sent the arrows of conviction to my soul." The other testimony was from a dying man: "Harriet, I am a lost man. You opposed our family worship and my secret prayer. You drew me away into temptation and to neglect every religious duty. I believe my fate is sealed. Harriet, you are the cause of my everlasting ruin." How many glorious married couples in heaven—Adam and Eve, Abraham and Sarah, Lapidoth and Deborah, Isaac and Rebekah, Jacob and Rachel, Zacharias and Elizabeth, Joseph and Mary, and many whom we have known as good as the most of them!

As once you stood in the village or city church or in your father's house, perhaps under a wedding-bell of flowers, to-day stand up, husband and wife, beneath the cross of a pardoning Redeemer, while I proclaim the banns of an eternal marriage. Join your right hands. I pronounce you one forever. The circle is an emblem of eternity, and that is the shape of the Wedding Ring.

FOOTNOTES:

[1] As Abigail did (1 Sam. 25:25).

COSTUME AND MORALS.ToC

"Moreover the Lord said, Because the daughters of Zion are haughty, and walk with stretched-forth necks and wanton eyes, walking and mincing as they go, and making a tinkling with their feet: in that day the Lord will take away the bravery of their tinkling ornaments about their feet, and their cauls, and their round tires like the moon, the chains, and the bracelets, and the mufflers, the bonnets, and the ornaments of the legs, and the headbands, and the tablets, and the earrings, the rings, and nose-jewels, the changeable suits of apparel, and the mantles, and the wimples, and the crisping pins, the glasses, and the fine linen, and the hoods, and the veils,"—ISAIAH 3:16, 18-23.[2]

This is a Jerusalem fashion plate. It puts us two thousand six hundred years back, and sets us down in an ancient city. The procession of men and women is moving up and down the gay streets. It is the height of the fashionable season. The sensible men and women move with so much modesty that they do not attract our attention. But here come the haughty daughters of Jerusalem! They lean forward; they lean very much forward—so far forward as to be unnatural—teetering, wobbling, wriggling, flirting, or, as my text describes it, they "walk with stretched-forth necks, walking and mincing as they go."

See! That is a princess. Look! That is a Damascus sword-maker. Look! That is a Syrian merchant. The jingling of the chains, and the lashing of the headbands, and the exhibitions of universal swagger attract the attention of the Prophet Isaiah, and he brings his camera to bear upon the scene, and takes a picture for all the ages. But where is that scene? Vanished. Where are those gay streets? Vermin-covered population pass through them. Where are the hands, and the necks, and the foreheads, and the shoulders, and the feet that sported all that magnificence? Ashes! Ashes!

That we should all be clad is proved by the opening of

THE FIRST WARDROBE

in Paradise, with its apparel of dark green. That we should all as far as our means allow us be beautifully and gracefully apparelled is proved by the fact that God never made a wave but He gilded it with golden sunbeams, or a tree but He garlanded it with blossoms, or a sky but He studded it with stars, or allowed even the smoke of a furnace to ascend but He columned, and turreted, and doled, and scrolled it into outlines of indescribable gracefulness. When I see the apple orchards of the spring and the pageantry of the autumnal forests, I come to the conclusion that if nature ever does join the Church, while she may be a Quaker in the silence of her worship, she never will be a Quaker in the style of her dress. Why the notches of a fern leaf or the stamen of a water lily? Why, when the day departs, does it let the folding doors of heaven stay open so long, when it might go in so quickly? One summer morning I saw an army of a million spears, each one adorned with a diamond of the first water—I mean the grass with the dew on it.

When the prodigal came home his father not only put a coat on his back, but jewelry on his hand. Christ wore a beard, Paul, the bachelor apostle, not afflicted with any sentimentality, admired the arrangement of a woman's hair, when he said in his epistle: "If a woman have long hair, it is a glory unto her." There will be fashion in heaven as on earth, but it will be a different kind of fashion. It will decide the color of the dress; and the population of that country, by a beautiful law, will wear white.

THE GODDESS OF FASHION.

I say these things as a background to my sermon, to show you that I have no prim, precise, prudish, or cast-iron theories on the subject of human apparel; but the goddess of fashion has set up her throne in this country and at the sound of the timbrels we are all expected to fall down and worship. Her altars smoke with the sacrifice of the bodies and souls of ten thousand victims.

When I come to count the victims of fashion I find as many masculine as feminine. Men make an easy tirade against woman, as though she were the chief worshipper at this idolatrous shrine, and no doubt some men in the more conspicuous part of the pew have already cast glances at the more retired part of the pew, their look a prophecy of a generous distribution. My sermon shall be as appropriate for one end of the pew as for the other.

MASCULINE FOLLIES.

Men are as much the idolaters of fashion as women, but they sacrifice on a different part of the altar. With men the fashion goes to cigars, and club-rooms, and yachting parties, and wine suppers. In the United States the men chew up and smoke one hundred millions of dollars' worth of tobacco every year. That is their fashion. In London not long ago a man died who started in life with $750,000; but he ate it all up in gluttonies, sending his agents to all parts of the earth for some rare delicacy for the palate, sometimes one plate of food costing him three or four hundred dollars. He ate up his whole fortune, and had only one guinea left. With that he bought a woodcock, and had it dressed in the very best style, ate it, gave two hours for digestion, then walked out on Westminster Bridge and threw himself into the Thames and died, doing on a large scale what you and I have often seen done on a small scale.

But men do not abstain from millinery and elaboration of skirt through any superiority of simplicity. It is only because such appendages would be a blockade to business. What would sashes and trains three and a half yards long do in a stock market? And yet men are the disciples of custom just as much as women. Some of them wear boots so tight that they can hardly walk in the paths of righteousness, and there are men who buy expensive suits of clothes and never pay for them, and who go through the streets in great stripes of color, like animated checkerboards. I say these things because I want to show you that I am impartial in my discourse, and that both sexes, in the language of the surrogate's office, "share and share alike."

INDELICATE APPAREL.

As God may help me I am going to set forth the evil effects of improper dress or an excessive discipleship of costume. It is a simple truth that you all know, although the pulpit has not yet uttered it, that much of the womanly costume of our time is the cause of the temporal and eternal damnation of a multitude of men. There is a shamelessness among many in what is called high life that calls for vehement protest. The strife with many seems to be how near they can come to the verge of indecency without falling over. The tide of masculine profligacy will never turn back until there is a decided reformation in womanly costume. I am in full sympathy with the officer of the law who, at a levee in Philadelphia last winter, went up to a so-called lady, and because of her sparse and incompetent apparel, ordered her either to leave the house or habilitate herself immediately. It is high time that our good and sensible women make vehement protest against fashionable indecency, and if the women of the household do not realize the deplorable extremes of much of the female costume, that husbands implead their wives on this subject, and that fathers prohibit their daughters. The evil is terrific and overshadowing.

STAGE COSTUMES.

I suppose that the American stage is responsible for much of this. I do not go to the theatres, so I must take the evidence of the actors and managers of theatres, such as Mr. John Gilbert, Mr. A.M. Palmer, and Mr. Daniel E. Bandmann. They have recently told us that the crime of undress is blasting the theatre, which by many is considered a school of morals, and indeed superior to the Church, and a forerunner of the millennium. Mr. Palmer says: "The bulk of the performances on the stage are degrading and pernicious. The managers strive to come just as near the line as possible without flagrantly breaking the law. There never have been costumes worn on a stage of this city, either in a theatre, hall, or 'dive,' so improper as those that clothe some of the chorus in recent comic opera productions." He says in regard to the female performers: "It is not a question whether they can sing, but just how little they will consent to wear." Mr. Bandmann, who has been twenty-nine years on the stage, and before almost all nationalities, says: "I unhesitatingly state that the taste of the present theatre-going people of America, as a body, is of a coarse and vulgar nature. The Hindoo would turn with disgust at such exhibitions, which are sought after and applauded on the stage of this country. Our shop windows are full of and the walls covered with show cards and posters which should be a disgrace to an enlightened country and an insult to the eye of a cultured community." Mr. Gilbert says: "Such exhibition is a disastrous one to the morals of the community. Are these proper pictures to put out for the public to look at, to say nothing of the propriety of females appearing in public dressed like that? It is shameful!"

I must take the testimony of the friends of the theatre and the confirmation which I see on the board fences and in the show windows containing the pictures of the way actresses dress. I suppose that those representations of play-house costume are true, for if they are not true, then those highly moral and religious theatres are swindling the public by inducing the people to the theatre by promises of spectacular nudity which they do not fulfill. Now, all this familiarizes the public with such improprieties of costume and depresses the public conscience as to what is allowable and right.

DRAWING-ROOM RIVALRY.

The parlor and drawing-room are now running a race with the theatre and opera bouffe. They are now nearly neck and neck in the race, the latter a little ahead; but the parlor and the drawing-room are gaining on the others, and the probability is they will soon be even and pass the stand so nearly at the same time that one half of Pandemonium will clap its hands because opera bouffe has beaten, and the other half because the drawing-room has beaten. Let printing-press, and platform, and pulpit hurl red-hot anathema at the boldness of much of womanly attire. I charge Christian women, neither by style of dress nor adjustment of apparel, to become administrative of evil. Show me the fashion plates of any age between this and the time of Louis XVI., of France, and Henry VIII., of England, and I will tell you the type of morals or immorals of that age or that year. No exception to it. Modest apparel means a righteous people. Immodest apparel always means a contaminated and depraved society.

EXTRAVAGANCE.

It is not only such boldness that is to be reprehended, but extravagance of costume. This latter is the cause of fraud unlimitable and ghastly. Do you know that Arnold of the Revolution proposed to sell his country in order to get money to support his home wardrobe? I declare here before God and this people that the effort to keep up expensive establishments in this country is sending more business men to temporal perdition than all other causes combined. It was this that sent prominent business men to the watering of stocks, and life insurance presidents to perjured statements about their assets, and some of them to the penitentiary, and has completely upset our American finances.

But why should I go to these famous defaultings, to show what men will do in order to keep up great home style and expensive wardrobe, when you and I know scores of men who are put to their wit's end and are lashed from January to December in the attempt? Our Washington politicians may theorize until the expiration of their terms of office as to the best way of improving our monetary condition in this country. It will be of no use, and things will be no better until we learn to put on our heads and backs and feet and hands no more than we can pay for.

AN INCENTIVE TO DISHONESTY.

There are clerks in stores and banks on limited salaries who in the vain attempt to keep the wardrobe of their family as showy as other folk's wardrobes are dying of muffs, and diamonds, and camel's-hair shawls, and high hats, and they have nothing left except what they give to cigars and wine suppers, and they die before their time, and they will expect us ministers to preach about them as though they were the victims of early piety; and after a high-class funeral, with silver handles at the side of their coffin of extraordinary brightness, it will be found out that the undertaker is cheated out of his legitimate expenses! Do not send to me to preach the funeral sermon of a man who dies like that. I would blurt out the whole truth, and tell that he was strangled to death by his wife's ribbons! The country is dressed to death.

You are not surprised to find that the putting up of one public building in New York cost millions of dollars more than it ought to have cost, when you find that the man who gave out the contracts paid more than five thousand dollars for his daughter's wedding dress. Cashmeres of a thousand dollars each are not rare on Broadway. It is estimated that there are eight thousand women in these two cities who have expended on their personal array two thousand dollars a year.

What are the men to do in order to keep up such home wardrobes? Steal—that is the only respectable thing they can do! During the last fifteen years there have been innumerable fine business men shipwrecked on the wardrobe. The temptation comes in this way: a man thinks more of his family than all the world outside, and if they spend the evening in describing to him the superior wardrobe of the family across the street that they cannot bear the sight of, the man is thrown on his gallantry and his pride of family, and without translating his feelings into plain language, he goes into extortion and issuing of false stock and skillful penmanship in writing somebody else's name at the foot of a promissory note; and they all go down together—the husband to the prison, the wife to the sewing machine, the children to be taken care of by those who were called poor relations. Oh, for some new Shakespeare to arise and write

THE TRAGEDY OF CLOTHES!

Act the first of the tragedy: A plain but beautiful home. Enter the newly married pair. Enter simplicity of manner and behavior. Enter as much happiness as is ever found in one home.

Act the second: Discontent with the humble home. Enter envy. Enter jealousy. Enter desire to display.

Act the third: Enlargement of expenses. Enter all the queenly dressmakers. Enter the French milliners.

Act the fourth: The tip-top of society. Enter princes and princesses of New York life. Enter magnificent plate and equipage. Enter everything splendid.

Act the fifth and last, winding up the scene: Enter the assignee. Enter the sheriff. Enter the creditors. Enter humiliation. Enter the wrath of God. Enter the contempt of society. Enter death. Now, let the silk curtain drop on the stage. The farce is ended, and the lights are out.

Will you forgive me if I say in tersest shape possible, that some of the men in this country have to forge, and to perjure, and to swindle to pay for their wives' dresses? I will say it whether you forgive me or not.

CURTAILS BENEVOLENCE.

Again, extravagant costume is the foe of all Christian alms-giving. Men and women put so much in personal display that they often have nothing for God and the cause of suffering humanity—a Christian man cracking his Palais Royal gloves across the back by shutting up his hand to hide the one cent he puts into the poor box! a Christian woman at the story of the Hottentots crying copious tears into a twenty-five dollar handkerchief, and then giving a two-cent piece to the collection, thrusting it down under the bills, so people will not know but it was a ten-dollar gold piece! One hundred dollars for incense to fashion—two cents for God! God gives us ninety cents out of every dollar. The other ten cents, by command of His Bible, belong to Him. Is not God liberal according to this tithing system laid down in the Old Testament—is not God liberal in giving us ninety cents out of a dollar when he takes but ten? We do not like that. We want to have ninety-nine cents for ourselves and one for God.

Now, I would a great deal rather steal ten cents from you than God. I think one reason why a great many people do not get along in worldly accumulation faster is because they do not observe this Divine rule. God says: "Well, if that man is not satisfied with ninety cents out of a dollar, then I will take the whole dollar, and I will give it to the man or woman who is honest with me." The greatest obstacle to charity in the Christian church to-day is the fact that men expend so much on their table, and women so much on their dress, they have got nothing left for the work of God and the world's betterment.

DISTRACTS ATTENTION.

Again, extravagant costume is distraction to a public worship. You know very well there are a good many people who go to church just as they go to the races, to see who will come out first. Men and women with souls to be saved passing the hour in wondering where that man got his cravat, or what store that woman patronizes. In many of our churches the preliminary exercises are taken up with the discussion of wardrobes. It is pitiable. Is it not wonderful that the Lord does not strike the meeting-houses with lightning? What distraction of public worship! Dying men and women, whose bodies are soon to be turned into dust, yet before three worlds strutting like peacocks. People sitting down in a pew or taking up a hymn book, all absorbed at the same time in personal array, to sing:

> "Rise, my soul, and stretch thy wings,
>   Thy better portion trace;
> Rise from transitory things
>   Toward heaven, thy native
>   place!"

I adopt the Episcopalian prayer, and say: "Good Lord, deliver us!"

MENTAL IMPOVERISHMENT.

Extravagant costume belittles the intellect. Our minds are enlarged or they dwindle just in proportion to the importance of the subject on which we constantly dwell. Can you imagine anything more dwarfing to the human intellect than the study of dress? I see men on the street who, judging from their elaboration, I think must have taken two hours to arrange their apparel. After a few years of that kind of absorption, which one of McAllister's magnifying glasses will be powerful enough to make the man's character visible? What will be left of a woman's intellect after giving years and years to the discussion of such questions? They all land in idiocy. I have seen men at the summer watering-places through fashion the mere wreck of what they once were. Sallow of cheek. Meagre of limb. Hollow at the chest. Showing no animation save in rushing across a room to pick up a lady's fan. Simpering along the corridors the same compliments they simpered twenty years ago.

BARS HEAVEN.

Yet, my friends, I have given you only the milder phase of this evil. It shuts a great multitude out of heaven. The first peal of thunder that shook Sinai declared: "Thou shalt have no other gods before me," and you will have to choose between the goddess of fashion and the Christian God. There are a great many seats in heaven, and they are all easy seats, but not one seat for the devotee of costume. Heaven is for meek and quiet spirits. Heaven is for those who think more of their souls than of their bodies.

Give up this idolatry of fashion or give up heaven. What would you do standing beside the Countess of Huntingdon, whose joy it was to build chapels for the poor; or with that Christian woman of Boston, who fed fifteen hundred children of the street, at Fanueil Hall, one New Year's Day, giving out as a sort of doxology at the end of the meeting a pair of shoes to each one of them; or those Dorcases of modern society who have consecrated their needles to the Lord, and who will get eternal reward for every stitch they take?

PERPETUAL ENVY.

Oh, men and women, give up the idolatry of costume! The rivalries and the competitions of such a life are a stupendous wretchedness. You will always find some one with brighter array, and with more palatial residence, and with lavender kid gloves that make a tighter fit. And if you buy this thing and wear it you will wish you had bought something else and worn it. And the frets of such a life will bring the crow's feet to your temples before they are due, and when you come to die you will have a miserable time.

I have seen men and women of excessive costume die, and I never saw one of them die well. The trappings off, there they lay on the tumbled pillow, and there were just two things that bothered them—a wasted life and a coming eternity. I could not pacify them, for their body, mind, and soul had been exhausted in the worship of costume, and they could not appreciate the Gospel. When I knelt by their bedside they were mumbling out their regrets, and saying: "O God! O God!" Their garments hung up in the wardrobe never again to be seen by them. Without any exception, so far as my memory serves me, they died without hope, and went into eternity unprepared. The two most ghastly death-beds on earth are the one where a man dies of delirium tremens, and the other where a woman dies after having sacrificed all her faculties of body, mind and soul in the worship of costume.

JUDGMENT TO COME.

My friends, we must appear in judgment to answer for what we have worn on our bodies as well as for what repentances we have exercised with our souls. On that day I see coming in Beau Brummell of the last century without his cloak; Aaron Burr, without the letters that to old age he showed in pride, to prove his early wicked gallantries; and Absalom without his hair; and Marchioness Pompadour without her titles; and Mrs. Arnold, the belle of Wall Street, when that was the centre of fashion, without her fripperies of vesture.

And in great haggardness they shall go away into eternal expatriation, while among the queens of heavenly society will be found Vashti, who wore the modest veil before the palatial bacchanalians; and Hannah, who annually made a little coat for Samuel at the temple; and Grandmother Lois, the ancestress of Timothy, who imitated her virtue; and Mary, who gave Jesus Christ to the world; and many of you, the wives, and mothers, and sisters, and daughters of the present Christian church who, through great tribulation, are entering into the kingdom of God. Christ announced who would make up the royal family of heaven when He said: "Whosoever doeth the will of God, the same is my brother, my sister, my mother."

FOOTNOTES:

[2] The list of feminine treasures given by the Revised Version is more intelligible. It is: "Their anklets, and the networks, and the crescents; the pendants, and the bracelets, and the mufflers; the head-tires, and the ankle chains, and the sashes, and the perfume boxes, and the amulets; the rings, and the nose-jewels; the festival robes, and the mantles, and the shawls, and the satchels; the hand-mirrors, and the fine linen, and the turbans, and the veils."

HUSBANDS AND WIVES.ToC

"Let every one in particular so love his wife even as himself; and the wife see that she reverence her husband."—EPHESIANS 5:33.

All this good advice by a man who never married. He lived on to fifty-eight years of age, in eminent bachelorhood. Indeed, it was better for Paul to remain in single life, because he went on such rapid missionary expeditions that no companion could have endured the hardship. Celibacy in some cases is better. Such persons accomplish under such circumstances that which could not be accomplished in the other style of life.

I have known men who remain unaffianced in order that they might take care of the children of a deceased brother; and what would become of the world without the self-sacrifice and helpfulness of the maiden aunts I cannot imagine.

Among the brightest queens of Heaven will be those who took care of other people's children. Alas for that household which has not within easy call an Aunt Mary! I know that there are caricatures, and ungallant things sometimes said; but so far as my observation goes, they are quite equal in disposition to their married sisters. The state of celibacy is honored again by such persons as Macaulay and Washington Irving in literature, and Florence Nightingale and Miss Dix in philanthropy.

But while Paul remained in the single state, he kept his eyes open, and he looked off upon the calm sea of married life, and upon the chopped sea of domestic perturbation. He comes forth in my text to say, "Let every one in particular so love his wife even as himself; and the wife see that she reverence her husband;" implying that the wife ought to be lovable, so there might be something to love, and the man ought to be honorable, so there might be something to reverence.

It is

A MOST CONGRATULATORY THOUGHT

that the vast majority of people in the married state are well mated. When the news is first announced in the outside world of the betrothal, there may be surprise and seeming incongruity, but as the years pass by it is demonstrated that the selection was divinely arranged. There may be great difference of temperament, great difference of appearance, great difference of circumstances. That is no objection. The sanguine and the phlegmatic temperaments make appropriate union, the blonde and the brunette, the quick and the slow, the French and the German. In the machinery of domestic life there is no more need for the driving wheel than for the brakes. That is the best union generally which has just the opposites.

The best argument in behalf of marriage as a divine institution is the fact that the vast majority of conjugal relationships are the very best things that could have happened. Once in a while there is a resounding exception to the good rule, the attempt being made to marry fire and gunpowder, with the consequent explosion in the divorce courts; but in the vast majority of instances the conjugal relation is a beautiful illustration of what the Psalmist said when he declared, "God setteth the solitary in families."

Taking it for granted, then, that you are well mated, I proceed to give you some

PRESCRIPTIONS FOR DOMESTIC HAPPINESS;

and, first of all, I remark:

I. A spirit of compromise must be dominant. You must remember that you were twenty or thirty years forming independent habits and having your own way. In the marriage state these habits must be brought into accord, and there may be some ingenuity necessary. Be determined to have your own way, and there will be no peace. Let the rule be: In all matters of moral principle your determination shall be iron, and in all unimportant matters, willow. Whatever you may think of the word compromise in politics, without compromise there is no domestic peace. A great many people are willing to compromise, if you will do just as they want you to do; but there is no compromise in that. The rule ought to be: In all domestic matters, all social matters, all ecclesiastical matters, all political matters, firm adherence to fundamentals, easy surrender in non-essentials. Be not too proud or too stubborn to give up. Compromise! Compromise!

II. I remark, again, that in order to domestic happiness there must be a spirit of

CONSULTATION.

The home ought to be a cabinet, where all the affairs of the household and all the affairs of business life come under comparison, inspection and advisal. That is an absurd rule we hear abroad in the world, that men ought never to take their business home. Ten thousand financial failures would have been avoided if men had consulted with their wives.

In the first place, woman has a capacity to judge of moral character which man has not. Before you invite into your business partnership any man, you ought to introduce him to your wife, and get her judgment as to his capacity and his integrity. After five minutes' conversation she will tell you as much about him as you will know at the close of twenty years, and perhaps you may find out too late.

A man proposes to come into your business partnership. You take him to your home. He tarries a little while, and is gone. You say to your wife, "Well, what do you think of him?" She says, "I don't like him at all." You say, "It's an absurd thing to form a prejudice against him on so short an acquaintance. I have known him for years, and I have never known any bad against him." "Well," she says, "I don't know why I have formed that opinion, but I tell you to beware. Put none of your financial interests in that man's keeping." Ten or fifteen years pass by. You come home some night and say, "Well, my dear, you are right; that man swindled me out of my last dollar." It is not because woman is wiser than man. It is because God has given her that peculiar intuition in regard to human character.

Now, you have no right to go into an enterprise which involves the homestead, or the education of your children, or the fate of your entire family, without home consultation. Of course, all this implies that you did not marry a fool. If at the marriage altar you committed suicide, you had better keep all your business affairs in your own heart and head. But let us hope that you have sound common sense presiding in your household.

A BEAUTIFUL INCIDENT.

How much a wife may help a husband's business affairs was well illustrated in the case where the wife saved from the allowance of herself and the allowance of the family, a certain amount of money for a rainy day. After some time the husband, coming home, said: "Well, I'm going to suspend payment to-morrow. A few dollars would get me through, but I can't get the few dollars, and I'm going to ruin." That evening the wife said: "I wish you would hunt up the definition of the word 'independence' in Webster's Dictionary. Hunt it up for me." He opened Webster's Dictionary, and found the word "independence," and right opposite was a $100 bill. "Now," she said, "I would like to have you find the word 'gratitude.'" He turned to the word "gratitude," and there was another $100 bill. And before the evening was past she asked him to read a verse of a certain chapter of the Bible. He opened to the verse in the Bible, and there were $500, and before the evening had passed, the man had financial relief to tide him over his disasters. You call that dramatic. I call that beautifully Christian.

In all expenditures there ought to be consultation. Do not dole out money to your wife as though she were a beggar. Let her know how much you have, or how little. Appeal to her intelligent judgment, and she will be content, and your own disposition will not be irritated. As long as you keep a mystery about your business matters she will wonder that the allowance is so small. No honorable woman wants to spend more money than can be afforded. Come into consultation with her on this matter. Show what are all your necessary outside expenses, all the money you have for cigars and dinners at Delmonico's, and how much it takes for the club-house and for the political campaign, and then have her present all the domestic expenses, and then, after consultation do your best.

It is a bad sign when a man dare not tell his business transactions to his wife. There is something wrong. Suppose you that the gigantic forgeries which have been enacted in this country would ever have taken place if the wife had been consulted? The wife would have said, "Stop! Let us live in one room in the poorest house on the poorest street of the poorest town, and have nothing but dry bread rather than that you should make yourself culpable before God and the law." In the vast majority of cases where there has been exposure of great frauds, the wife has been the most surprised person in the community.

A BANKER

some time ago misused trust funds, and he went from fraud to fraud, and from knavery to knavery, until it was necessary for him to leave home before daylight. His wife said: "Where are you going?" "I am going to New York," said he "I am going on the early train." "Why, isn't this sudden?" she asked. "Oh, no; I expected to go," and then he left the room and went up to the room where his daughters slept, looked upon their calm faces for the last time, as he supposed, and started. He was brought back by the constables of an outraged law, and is now in the penitentiary.

Do you suppose that man, with a good wife, as he had, an honest wife, as he had, a Christian wife, as he had, could have got into such an enormity if he had consulted in regard to her wishes? Consultation is the word—domestic consultation.

III. Again: in order to domestic happiness, there must, in the conjugal state, be

NO SECRETS

kept one from the other. What one knows both must know. It is a bad sign when one partner in the conjugal relation is afraid to have the letters opened or read by the other partner. Surreptitious correspondence is always dangerous. If a man comes to you and says, "I am going to tell you a great privacy, and don't want you to tell anybody, not even your wife," say to him, "Well, now, you had better not tell me, for I shall tell her as soon as I get home."

There must be no secrecy of association. You ought not to be unwilling to tell where you have been, and with whom you have been. Sometimes an unwise wife will have a lady confidante whom she makes a depository of privacies which they are pledged to keep between themselves. Beware! Anything that implies that husband and wife are two and not one implies peril, domestic peril, social peril, mighty peril.

In the vast majority of cases of domestic infelicity coming to exposure in the courts, the trouble began by the accidental opening of a letter which implied correspondence which was never suspected. In the conjugal relations, secrets kept one from another are nitro-glycerine under the hearthstone, and the fuse is lighted!

IV. Again: in order to your happiness there must be a spirit of

FORBEARANCE.

In the weeks, the months, the years that you were planning for each other's conquest, only the more genial side of your nature was observable, but now you are off guard, and the faults are all known the one to the other. You are aware of your imperfections, unless you are one of those self-conceited people who are quickly observant of faults in others, but oblivious to faults in yourself; and now having found out all of each others imperfections, forbear.

If the one be given to too much precision, and the other disorderly in habits; if the one be spendthrift and the other oversaving; if the one be loquacious, and the other reticent, forbear. Especially, if you both have inflammable tempers, do not both get mad at once. Take turn about! William Cowper put it well when he said:

> "The kindest and the happiest pair
> Will find occasion to forbear;
> And something every day they live
> To pity, and perhaps forgive."

V. Again: in order to your happiness, let there be no interfering with each other's peculiar

RELIGIOUS SENTIMENTS.

If you are a Baptist and your wife a Pedo-Baptist, do not go to splashing water into each other's faces! If you are a Presbyterian and your husband is a Methodist, when he shouts "Hallelujah!" do not get nervous.

If you have strong denominational proclivities, one of you had better go to one church, and the other had better go to another church; or, surrendering some of your intensity on that subject, as in hundreds of cases, come to some such church as the Brooklyn Tabernacle, where, while we adhere to the fundamentals of the Gospel, we do not care a rye straw for the infinitesimal differences between evangelical denominations—putting one drop of water on the brow, if that is enough baptism, and if not, then plunging the candidate clear out of sight, if that is preferred—not caring whether you believe you have been foreordained to be saved or not, if you are only saved; nor whether you believe in the perseverance of the saints or not, if you will only persevere; nor whether you prefer prayer by Episcopal liturgy or extemporaneous supplication, if you only pray.

Do not let there be any religious contests across the breakfast table or the tea table. It makes but little difference from what direction you come toward the riven heart of Christ, if you only come up to the riven heart. Yet, I know in many families there is constant picking at opposite religious beliefs, and attempt at proselytism. You, the father, fight for Episcopacy, and you, the mother, fight for Presbyterianism, and your children will compromise the matter and be Nothingarians!

VI. Again: I counsel you, in order to your domestic happiness, that you

CULTIVATE EACH OTHER'S RELIGIOUS WELFARE.

This is a profoundly agitating thought to every fair-minded man and woman. You live, together on earth; you want to live together forever. You do not want ten, or twenty, or fifty years to end your association, you want to take your companion into the kingdom of God with you. If this subject is irritating in the household, it is because you do not understand Christian stratagem.

Every Christian companion may take his or her companion into glory. How? Ask God, and he will tell you how. Perhaps by occasional religious remark. Perhaps by earnest prayer. Perhaps by a consistent life. More probably by all these things combined. Paul put it forcefully when he said: "How knowest thou, O wife, whether thou shalt save thy husband? how knowest thou, O man, whether thou shalt save thy wife?" In this house, how many have been remarried for the skies!

It has become so much the general rule that when in my congregation, as I often do, I find a family in which the wife is a Christian, and the husband is not, I just say frankly to him: "Now you have got to come in. You might just as well try to swim up against Niagara rapids as against the tide of religious influence which in this church is going to surge you into the kingdom of God. You must come in. You know that your wife is right in this matter of religion. She may be quick of temper, and you may sometimes lose your patience with her, but you know she is better than you are, and you know when she dies she will go as straight to heaven as a shot to a target.

"And, if to-day, on the way home, a vehicle should dash down the street, and she should fall lifeless, with no opportunity for last words, you might have a doubt about what would become of you, and a doubt about what would become of the children, but you would have no doubt about her eternal destiny. Somewhere under the flush of her cheek, or under the pallor of her brow is the Lord's mark. She is your wife, but she is God's child, and you are not jealous of that relationship. You only wish that you yourself were a son of the Lord Almighty. Come and have the matter settled. If I die before you, I will not forget in the next world how you stood together here, but I will expect both of you. You must come.

"I say it in all Christian love and emphasis, as a brother talks to a brother. You must come. You have been united so long, you cannot afford to have death divorce you. How long it is since you began the struggle of life together! You have helped each other on the road, and what you have done for each other God only knows. There have been tedious sicknesses, and anxious watching, and here and there a grave, short but very deep; and though the blossoms of the marriage day may have scattered, and the lips that pronounced you one may have gone into dust, you have through all these years been to each other true as steel.

"Now, to-day, I am going to remarry you for heaven. This is the bridal day of your soul's peace. Here is the marriage altar. Kneel side by side, take the oath of eternal fidelity, clasp hands in a covenant never to be broken. I pronounce you one on earth, I pronounce you one for eternity. What God by His grace hath joined together, let not earth or hell put asunder. Hark! I hear a humming in the air—an anthem—a wedding march—organs celestial played upon by fingers seraphic."

I do not think I ever read anything more beautiful and quaintly pathetic than

COTTON MATHER'S DESCRIPTION

of the departure of his wife from earth to Heaven: "The black day arrives. I had never seen so black a day in all the time of my pilgrimage. The desire of my eyes is this day to be taken from me at a stroke. Her death is lingering and painful. All the forenoon of this day she was in the pangs of death, and sensible until the last minute or two before her final expiration. I cannot remember the discourse that passed between us, only her devout soul was full of satisfaction about her going to a state of blessedness with the Lord Jesus Christ. As far as my distress would permit, I studied to confirm her satisfaction and consolation.

"When I saw to what a point of resignation I was called of the Lord, I resolved, with His help, to glorify Him. So, two hours before she expired, I knelt by her bedside and took into my hands that dear hand, the dearest in the world, and solemnly and sincerely gave her up to the Lord. I gently put her out of my hands and laid away her hand, resolved that I would not touch it again. She afterward told me that she signed and sealed my act of resignation, and though before that she had called for me continually, after it she never asked for me any more. She conversed much until near two in the afternoon. The last sensible word she spoke was to her weeping father: 'Heaven, Heaven will make amends for all!'"

Now let us be faithful in this relation of which I have been speaking. Do you want to know

WHAT THE LORD THINKS OF IT?

Read the sixty-second chapter of Isaiah, where he says: "As the bridegroom rejoiceth over the bride, so shall thy God rejoice over thee." There is a wedding coming which will eclipse all the princely and imperial weddings the world ever saw. It was a great day when Napoleon took Josephine; it was a great day when Henry VIII. led Anne Boleyn over the cloth of gold on the street, the cloth of gold reaching up to the palace; it was a great day when the King of Spain took Mercedes; but there will be a greater time when the Lord shall take His bride, the Church, to Himself.

Long time ago they were affianced, but she has been down in the wilderness. He has written her again and again, and the day of marriage is fixed. She has sent word to Him. He has sent word to her. But, oh! was there ever such a difference in estate? The King on the one side, the bride of the wilderness, poor and persecuted, on the other. The wealth of the universe on the one side, the obscurity of the ages on the other. The pomp of heaven on the one side, the poverty of earth on the other. But He will endow her with all His wealth, and raise her to sit with Him on a throne forever.

Come, thou bridal morn of the ages! Come! and there shall be the rumbling of great wheels, great chariot wheels down the sky, and there shall be riders ahead and mounted cavalry behind, the conquerors of heaven on white horses. Clear the way! A thousand trumpets blare. "Behold! the bridegroom cometh: go ye out to meet Him."

Then the charioteers shall rein in their bounding steeds of fire, and the King shall dismount from the chariot, and He shall take by the hand the bride of the wilderness, all the crowded galleries of the universe, the spectators. Ring all the wedding bells of heaven. The King lifts the bride into the chariot and cries, "Drive on! drive up!" and the clouds shall spread their cloth of gold for the procession, and the twain shall go through the gates triumphant, and up the streets, and then step into the palace at the banquet, where ten thousand potentates and principalities and dominations, cherubic and archangelic, with ten thousand gleaming and uplifted chalices, shall celebrate the day when the King of Heaven and earth brings home His bride from the wilderness. Make haste, my beloved. Be thou like to a roe, or a young hart upon the mountains of spices.

MATRIMONIAL DISCORDS.ToC

"Can two walk together, except they be agreed?"—Amos 3:3.

A church within a church, a republic within a republic, a world within a world, is spelled by four letters—Home! If things go right there, they go right everywhere; if things go wrong there, they go wrong everywhere. The door-sill of the dwelling-house is the foundation of Church and State. A man never gets higher than his own garret or lower than his own cellar. In other words, domestic life overarches and undergirds all other life. The highest House of Congress is the domestic circle; the rocking-chair in the nursery is higher than a throne. George Washington commanded the forces of the United States, but Mary Washington commanded George. Chrysostom's mother made his pen for him. If a man should start out and run seventy years in a straight line he could not get out from under the shadow of his own mantelpiece. I therefore talk to you this morning about a matter of infinite and eternal moment when I speak of your home.

THE SOCIAL BALANCE.

As individuals we are fragments. God makes the race in part, and then he gradually puts us together. What I lack, you make up; what you lack, I make up; our deficits and surpluses of character being the cog-wheels in the great social mechanism. One person has the patience, another has the courage, another has the placidity, another has the enthusiasm; that which is lacking in one is made up by another, or made up by all. Buffaloes in herds, grouse in broods, quail in flocks, the human race in circles. God has most beautifully arranged this. It is in this way that he balances society; this conservative and that radical keeping things even. Every ship must have its mast, cutwater, taffrail, ballast. Thank God, then, for Princeton and Andover, for the opposites.

I have no more right to blame a man for being different from me than a driving-wheel has a right to blame the iron shaft that holds it to the centre. John Wesley balances Calvin's Institutes. A cold thinker gives to Scotland the strong bones of theology; Dr. Guthrie clothes them with a throbbing heart and warm flesh. The difficulty is that we are not satisfied with just the work that God has given us to do. The water-wheel wants to come inside the mill and grind the grist, and the hopper wants to go out and dabble in the water. Our usefulness and the welfare of society depend upon our staying in just the place that God has put us, or intended we should occupy.

A RELIC OF EDEN.

For more compactness and that we may be more useful we are gathered in still smaller circles in the home group. And there you have the same varieties again; brothers, sisters, husband and wife; all different in temperaments and tastes. It is fortunate that it should be so. If the husband be all impulse, the wife must be all prudence. If one sister be sanguine in her temperament, the other must be lymphatic. Mary and Martha are necessities. There will be no dinner for Christ if there be no Martha; there will be no audience for Jesus if there be no Mary. The home organization is most beautifully constructed. Eden has gone; the bowers are all broken down; the animals that Adam stroked with his hand that morning when they came up to get their names have since shot forth tusk and sting and growled, panther at panther; in mid-air iron beaks plunge till with clotted wing and eyeless sockets the twain come whirling down from under the sun in blood and fire. Eden has gone, but there is just one little fragment left. It floated down on the River Hiddekel out of Paradise. It is the marriage institution. It does not, as at the beginning, take away from man a rib. Now it is an addition of ribs.

THE HOME ASSAULTED.

This institution of marriage has been defamed in our day, and influences are abroad trying to turn this earth into a Turkish harem or a great Salt Lake City. While the pulpits have been comparatively silent, novels—their cheapness only equalled by their nastiness—are trying to educate, have taken upon themselves to educate, this nation in regard to holy marriage, which makes or breaks for time and eternity. Oh, this is not a mere question of residence or wardrobe! It is a question charged with gigantic joy or sorrow, with heaven or hell. Alas for this new dispensation of George Sands! Alas for the mingling of the nightshade with the marriage garlands! Alas for the venom of adders spit into the tankards! Alas for the white frosts of eternal death that kill the orange blossoms! The Gospel of Jesus Christ is to assert what is right and to assert what is wrong.

THE ASSAULT OF THE SORDID.

Attempt has been made to take the marriage institution, which was intended for the happiness and elevation of the race, and make it a mere commercial enterprise; an exchange of houses and lands and equipage; a business partnership of two, stuffed up with the stories of romance and knight-errantry, and unfaithfulness and feminine angelhood. The two after a while have roused up to find that, instead of the paradise they dreamed of, they have got nothing but a Van Amburgh's menagerie, filled with tigers and wild-cats. Twenty thousand divorces in Paris in one year preceded the worst revolution that France ever saw. It was only the first course in that banquet of hell; and I tell you what you know as well as I do, that wrong notions on the subject of Christian marriage are the cause at this day of more moral outrage before God and man than any other cause.

There are some things that I want to bring before you. I know there are those of you who have had homes set up for a great many years; and then there are those here who have just established their home. They have only been in it a few months or a few years. Then there are those who will, after awhile, set up for themselves a home, and it is right that I should speak out upon these themes.

THE BENEFICENT GUEST.

My first counsel to you is, have Jesus in your new home, if it be a new home, and let Him who was a guest at Bethany be in your household; let the divine blessing drop upon your every hope and plan and expectation. Those young people who begin with God end with heaven. Have on your right hand the engagement ring of the divine affection. If one of you be a Christian, let that one take a Bible and read a few verses in the evening-time, and then kneel down and commend yourselves to Him who setteth the solitary in families. I want to tell you that the destroying angel passes by without touching or entering the door-post sprinkled with the blood of the everlasting covenant. Why is it that in some families they never get along, and in others they always get along well? I have watched such cases, and have come to a conclusion. In the first instance, nothing seemed to go pleasantly, and after awhile came devastation, domestic disaster or estrangement. Why? They started wrong! In the other case, although there were hardships and trials, and some things that had to be explained, still things went on pleasantly until the very last. Why? They started right!

FORBEARANCE NEEDED.

My advice to you in your home is to exercise to the very last possibility of your nature the law of forbearance. Prayers in the household will not make up for everything. Some of the best people in the world are the hardest to get along with. There are people who stand up in prayer-meetings and pray like angels, who at home are uncompromising and cranky. You may not have everything just as you want it. Sometimes it will be the duty of the husband, and sometimes of the wife, to yield; but both stand punctiliously on your rights, and you will have a Waterloo with no Blucher coming up at nightfall to decide the conflict.

A GRANDFATHER'S APOLOGY.

Never be ashamed to apologize when you have done wrong in domestic affairs. Let that be a law of your household. The best thing I ever heard of my grandfather, whom I never saw, was this: that once, having unrighteously rebuked one of his children, he himself having lost his patience, and, perhaps, having been misinformed of the child's doings, found out his mistake, and in the evening of the same day gathered all his family together, and said: "Now I have one explanation to make, and one thing to say. Thomas, this morning, I rebuked you very unfairly. I am very sorry for it. I rebuked you in the presence of the whole family, and now I ask your forgiveness in their presence." It must have taken some courage to do that. It was right, was it not? Never be ashamed to apologize for domestic inaccuracy. Find out the points; what are the weak points, if I may call them so, of your companion, and then stand aloof from them.

Do not carry the fire of your temper too near the gunpowder. If the wife be easily fretted by disorder in the household, let the husband be careful where he throws his slippers. If the husband come home from the store with his patience all exhausted, do not let the wife unnecessarily cross his temper; but both stand up for your rights, and I will promise the everlasting sound of the war-whoop. Your life will be spent in making up, and marriage will be to you an unmitigated curse. Cowper said:

> "The kindest and the happiest pair
> Will find occasion to forbear;
> And something every day they live,
> To pity, and perhaps forgive."

I advise, also, that you make your chief pleasure circle around about that home. It is unfortunate when it is otherwise. If the husband spend the most of his nights away from home, of choice, and not of necessity, he is not the head of the household; he is only the cashier. If the wife throw the cares of the household in the servant's lap, and then spend five nights of the week at the opera or theatre, she may clothe her children with satins and laces and ribbons that would confound a French milliner, but they are orphans. Oh, it is sad when a child has to say its prayers alone because mother has gone off to the evening entertainment! In India they bring children and throw them to the crocodiles, and it seems very cruel; but the jaws of New York and Brooklyn dissipation are swallowing down more little children to-day than all the monsters that ever crawled upon the banks of the Ganges!

A GODLESS MOTHER'S GRIEF.

I have seen the sorrow of a godless mother on the death of a child she had neglected. It was not so much grief that she felt from the fact that the child was dead as the fact that she had neglected it. She said: "If I had only watched over and cared for the child, I know God would not have taken it." The tears came not; it was a dry, blistering tempest—a scorching simoon of the desert. When she wrung her hands it seemed as if she would twist her fingers from their sockets; when she seized her hair it seemed as if she had, in wild terror, grasped a coiling serpent with her right hand.

No tears! Comrades of the little one came in and wept over the coffin; neighbors came in, and the moment they saw the still face of the child the shower broke. No tears for her. God gives tears as the summer rain to the parched soul; but in all the universe the driest and hottest, the most scorching and consuming thing is a mother's heart if she has neglected her child, when once it is dead. God may forgive her, but she will never forgive herself. The memory will sink the eyes deeper into the sockets, and pinch the face, and whiten the hair, and eat up the heart with vultures that will not be satisfied, forever plunging deeper their iron beaks. Oh, you wanderers from your home, go back to your duty! The brightest flowers in all the earth are those which grow in the garden of a Christian household, clambering over the porch of a Christian home.

MATRIMONIAL CONGENIALITY.

I advise you also to cultivate sympathy of occupation. Sir James Mackintosh, one of the most eminent and elegant men that ever lived, while standing at the very height of his eminence, said to a great company of scholars: "My wife made me." The wife ought to be the advising partner in every firm. She ought to be interested in all the losses and gains of shop and store. She ought to have a right—she has a right—to know everything. If a man goes into a business transaction that he dare not tell his wife of, you may depend that he is on the way either to bankruptcy or moral ruin. There may be some things which he does not wish to trouble his wife with; but if he dare not tell her, he is on the road to discomfiture.

On the other hand, the husband ought to be sympathetic with the wife's occupation. It is no easy thing to keep house. Many a woman that could have endured martyrdom as well as Margaret, the Scotch girl, has actually been worn out by house management. There are a thousand martyrs of the kitchen. It is very annoying, after the vexations of the day, around the stove or the table, or in the nursery or parlor, to have your husband say: "You know nothing about trouble; you ought to be in the store half an hour." Sympathy of occupation!

If the husband's work cover him with the soot of the furnace or the odors of leather or soap factories, let not the wife be easily disgusted at the begrimed hands or unsavory aroma. Your gains are one, your interests are one, your losses are one; lay hold of the work of life with both hands. Four hands to fight the battles; four eyes to watch for the danger; four shoulders on which to carry the trials. It is a very sad thing when the painter has a wife who does not like pictures. It is a very sad thing for a pianist when she has a husband who does not like music.

GENTEEL BUSINESS.

It is a very sad thing when a wife is not suited unless her husband has what is called a "genteel business." So far as I understand a "genteel business," it is something to which a man goes at ten o'clock in the morning, and from which he comes home at two or three o'clock in the afternoon, and gets a large amount of money for doing nothing. That is, I believe, a "genteel business;" and there has been many a wife who has made the mistake of not being satisfied until the husband has given up the tanning of the hides, or the turning of the banisters, or the building of the walls, and put himself in circles where he has nothing to do but smoke cigars and drink wine, and get himself into habits that upset him, going down in the maelstrom, taking his wife and children with him.

There are a good many trains running from earth to destruction. They start all the hours of the day, and all the hours of the night. There are the freight trains; they go very slowly and very heavily; and there are the accommodation trains going on toward destruction, and they stop very often and let a man get out when he wants to. But genteel idleness is an express train; Satan is the stoker, and Death is the engineer; and though one may come out in front of it and swing the red flag of "danger," or the lantern of God's Word, it makes just one shot into perdition, coming down the embankment with a shout and a wail and a shriek—crash, crash! There are two classes of people sure of destruction: First, those who have nothing to do; secondly, those who have something to do, but are too lazy or too proud to do it.

LOVE TO PRESIDE.

I have one more word of advice to give to those who would have a happy home, and that is, let love preside in it. When your behavior in the domestic circle becomes a mere matter of calculation; when the caress you give is merely the result of deliberate study of the position you occupy, happiness lies stark dead on the hearthstone. When the husband's position as head of the household is maintained by loudness of voice, by strength of arm, by fire of temper, the republic of domestic bliss has become a despotism that neither God nor man will abide. Oh, ye who promised to love each other at the altar, how dare you commit perjury? Let no shadow of suspicion come on your affection. It is easier to kill that flower than it is to make it live again. The blast from hell that puts out that light leaves you in the blackness of darkness forever.

A HOUSE NOT A HOME.

Here are a man and wife; they agree in nothing else, but they agree they will have a home. They will have a splendid house, and they think that if they have a house they will have a home. Architects make the plan, and the mechanics execute it; the house to cost one hundred thousand dollars. It is done. The carpets are spread, lights are hoisted, curtains are hung, cards of invitation sent out. The horses in gold-plated harness prance at the gate; guests come in and take their places; the flute sounds; the dancers go up and down; and with one grand whirl the wealth and the fashion and the mirth of the great town wheel amidst the pictured walls.

Ha! this is happiness. Float it on the smoking viands; sound it in the music; whirl it in the dance; cast it on the snow of sculpture; sound it up the brilliant stairway; flash it in chandeliers! Happiness, indeed! Let us build on the centre of the parlor floor a throne to Happiness; let all the guests, when they come in, bring their flowers and pearls and diamonds, and throw them on this pyramid, and let it be a throne; and then let Happiness, the Queen, mount the throne, and we will stand around and, all chalices lifted, we will say: "Drink, O Queen! live forever!"

LIGHTS OUT.

But the guests depart, the flutes are breathless, the last clash of the impatient hoofs is heard in the distance, and the twain of the household come back to see the Queen of Happiness on the throne amid the parlor floor. But, alas! as they come back the flowers have faded, the sweet odors have become the smell of a charnel-house, and instead of the Queen of Happiness there sits there the gaunt form of Anguish, with bitten lip and sunken eye, and ashes in her hair.

The romp and joyous step of the dancers who have left seems rumbling yet, like jarring thunders that quake the floor and rattle the glasses of the feast, rim to rim. The spilled wine on the floor turns into blood. The wreaths of plush have become wriggling reptiles. Terrors catch tangled in the canopy that overhangs the couch. A strong gust of wind comes through the hall and the drawing-room and the bed-chamber, in which all the lights go out. And from the lips of the wine-beakers come the words: "Happiness is not in us!" And the arches respond: "It is not in us!" And the silenced instruments of music, thrummed on by invisible fingers, answer: "Happiness is not in us!" And the frozen lips of Anguish break open, and, seated on the throne of wilted flowers, she strikes her bony hands together, and groans: "It is not in me!"

HAPPINESS IN POVERTY.

That very night a clerk with a salary of a thousand dollars a year—only one thousand—goes to his home, set up three months ago, just after the marriage-day. Love meets him at the door; love sits with him at the table; love talks over the work of the day; love takes down the Bible, and reads of Him who came our souls to save; and they kneel, and while they are kneeling—right in that plain room, on that plain carpet—the angels of God build a throne, not out of flowers that perish and fade away, but out of garlands of heaven, wreath on top of wreath, amaranth on amaranth, until the throne is done. Then the harps of God sounded, and suddenly there appeared one who mounted the throne, with eye so bright and brow so fair that the twain knew it was Christian Love. And they knelt at the throne, and, putting one hand on each head, she blessed them, and said: "Happiness is with me!" And that throne of celestial bloom withered not with the passing years; and the queen left not the throne till one day the married pair felt stricken in years—felt themselves called away, and knew not which way to go, and the queen bounded from the throne, and said: "Follow me, and I will show you the way up to the realm of everlasting love." And so they went up to sing songs of love, and walk on pavements of love, and to live together in mansions of love, and to rejoice forever in the truth that God is love.

HOTELS VERSUS HOMES.ToC

> "And brought him to an inn, and took care of him. And on the morrow when he departed, he took out two pence, and gave them to the host, and said unto him, Take care of him; and whatsoever thou spendest more, when I come again, I will repay thee."—LUKE 10:34, 35.

This is the good Samaritan paying the hotel bill of a man who had been robbed and almost killed by bandits. The good Samaritan had found the unfortunate on a lonely, rocky road, where, to this very day, depredations are sometimes committed upon travelers, and had put the injured man into the saddle, while this merciful and well-to-do man had walked till they got to the hotel, and the wounded man was put to bed and cared for. It must have been a very superior hotel in its accommodations, for, though in the country, the landlord was paid at the rate of what in our country would be four or five dollars a day, a penny being then a day's wages, and the two pennies paid in this case about two days' wages. Moreover, it was one of those kind-hearted landlords who are wrapped up in the happiness of their guests, because the good Samaritan leaves the poor wounded fellow to his entire care, promising that when he came that way again he would pay all the bills until the invalid got well.

THE VALUE OF HOTELS.

Hotels and boarding-houses are necessities. In very ancient times they were unknown, because the world had comparatively few inhabitants, who were not much given to travel, and private hospitality met all the wants of sojourners, as when Abraham rushed out at Mamre to invite the three men to sit down to a dinner of veal; as when the people were positively commanded to be given to hospitality; as in many of the places in the East these ancient customs are practiced to-day. But we have now hotels presided over by good landlords, and boarding-houses presided over by excellent host or hostess, in all neighborhoods, villages and cities, and it is our congratulation that those of our land surpass all other lands. They rightly become the permanent residences of many people, such as those who are without families, such as those whose business keeps them migratory, such as those who ought not, for various reasons of health or peculiarity of circumstances, take upon themselves the cares of housekeeping.

QUEENLY CATERERS.

Many a man falling sick in one of these boarding-houses or hotels has been kindly watched and nursed; and by the memory of her own sufferings and losses the lady at the head of such a house has done all that a mother could do for a sick child, and the slumberless eye of God sees and appreciates her sacrifices in behalf of the stranger. Among the most marvelous cases of patience and Christian fidelity are many of those who keep boarding-houses, enduring without resentment the unreasonable demands of their guests for expensive food and attentions for which they are not willing to pay an equivalent—a lot of cranky men and women who are not worthy to tie the shoe of their queenly caterer. The outrageous way in which boarders sometimes act to their landlords and landladies show that these critical guests had bad early rearing, and that in the making-up of their natures all that constitutes the gentleman and lady were left out. Some of the most princely men and some of the most elegant women that I know of to-day keep hotels and boarding-houses.

But one of the great evils of this day is found in the fact that a large population of our towns and cities are giving up and have given up their homes and taken apartments, that they may have more freedom from domestic duties and more time for social life, and because they like the whirl of publicity better than the quiet and privacy of a residence they can call their own. The lawful use of these hotels and boarding-houses is for most people while they are in transitu: but as a terminus they are in many cases demoralization, utter and complete. That is the point at which families innumerable have begun to disintegrate. There never has been a time when so many families, healthy and abundantly able to support and direct homes of their own, have struck tent and taken permanent abode in these public establishments. It is an evil wide as Christendom, and by voice and through the newspaper press I utter warning and burning protest, and ask Almighty God to bless the word, whether in the hearing or reading.

PROMOTERS OF GOSSIP.

In these public caravanseries the demon of gossip is apt to get full sway. All the boarders run daily the gauntlet of general inspection—how they look when they come down in the morning and when they get in at night, and what they do for a living, and whom they receive as guests in their rooms, and what they wear, and what they do not wear, and how they eat, and what they eat, and how much they eat, and how little they eat. If a man proposes in such a place to be isolated and reticent and alone, they will begin to guess about him: Who is he? Where did he come from? How long is he going to stay? Has he paid his board? How much does he pay? Perhaps he has committed some crime and does not want it to be known; there must be something wrong about him, or he would speak.

The whole house goes into the detective business. They must find out about him. They must find out about him right away. If he leave his door unlocked by accident he will find that his rooms have been inspected, his trunk explored, his letters folded differently from the way they were folded when he put them away. Who is he? is the question, asked with intenser interest, until the subject has become a monomania. The simple fact is, that he is nobody in particular, but minds his own business. The best landlords and landladies cannot sometimes hinder their places from becoming

A PANDEMONIUM

of whisperers, and reputations are torn to tatters, and evil suspicions are aroused, and scandals started, and the parliament of the family is blown to atoms by some Guy Fawkes who was not caught in time, as was his English predecessor of gunpowdery reputation.

The reason is that while in private homes families have so much to keep them busy, in these promiscuous and multitudinous residences there are so many who have nothing to do, and that always makes mischief. They gather in each other's rooms and spend hours in consultation about others. If they had to walk a half mile before they got to the willing ear of some listener to detraction they would get out of breath before reaching there, and not feel in full glow of animosity or slander, or might, because of the distance, not go at all. But rooms 20, 21, 22, 23, 24 and 25 are on the same corridor, and when one carrion crow goes "Caw! Caw!" all the other crows hear it and flock together over the same carcass. "Oh, I have heard something rich! Sit down and let me tell you all about it." And the first guffaw increases the gathering, and it has to be told all over again, and as they separate each carries a spark from the altar of Gab to some other circle, until from the coal-heaver in the cellar to the maid in the top room of the garret all are aware of the defamation, and that evening all who leave the house will bear it to other houses, until autumnal fires sweeping across Illinois prairies are less raging and swift than that flame of consuming reputation blazing across the village or city.

Those of us who were brought up in the country know that the old-fashioned hatching of eggs in the hay-mow required four or five weeks of brooding, but there are new modes of hatching by machinery, which take less time and do the work in wholesale. So, while the private home may brood into life an occasional falsity, and take a long time to do it, many of the boarding-houses and family hotels afford a swifter and more multitudinous style of moral incubation, and one old gossip will get off the nest after one hour's brooding, clucking a flock of thirty lies after her, each one picking up its little worm of juicy regalement. It is no advantage to hear too much about your neighbors, for your time will be so much occupied in taking care of their faults that you will have no time to look after your own. And while you are pulling the chickweed out of their garden yours will get all overgrown with horse-sorrel and mullen stalks.

A WRONG TO CHILDREN.

One of the worst damages that comes from the herding of so many people into boarding-houses and family hotels is inflicted upon children. It is only another way of bringing them up on the commons. While you have your own private house you can, for the most part, control their companionship and their whereabouts; but by twelve years of age in these public resorts they will have picked up all the bad things that can be furnished by the prurient minds of dozens of people. They will overhear blasphemies, and see quarrels, and get precocious in sin, and what the bartender does not tell them the porter or hostler or bell-boy will.

Beside that, the children will go out into this world without the restraining, anchoring, steadying and all-controlling memory of a home. From that none of us who have been blessed of such memory have escaped. It grips a man for eighty years, if he lives so long. It pulls him back from doors into which he otherwise would enter. It smites him with contrition in the very midst of his dissipations. As the fish already surrounded by

THE LONG WIDE NET

swim out to sea, thinking they can go as far as they please, and with gay toss of silvery scale they defy the sportsman on the beach, and after a while the fishermen begin to draw in the net, hand over hand, and hand over hand, and it is a long while before the captured fins begin to feel the net, and then they dart this way and that, hoping to get out, but find themselves approaching the shore, and are brought up to the very feet of the captors, so the memory of an early home sometimes seems to relax and let men out further and further from God and further and further from shore—five years, ten years, twenty years, thirty years; but some day they find an irresistible mesh drawing them back, and they are compelled to retreat from their prodigality and wandering; and though they make desperate effort to escape the impression, and try to dive deeper down in sin, after a while are brought clear back and held upon the Rock of Ages.

If it be possible, O father and mother! let your sons and daughters go out into the world under the semi-omnipotent memory of a good, pure home. About your two or three rooms in a boarding-house or a family hotel you can cast no such glorious sanctity. They will think of these public caravanseries as an early stopping place, malodorous with old victuals, coffees perpetually steaming, and meats in everlasting stew or broil, the air surcharged with carbonic acid, and corridors along which drunken boarders come staggering at one o'clock in the morning, rapping at the door till the affrighted wife lets them in. Do not be guilty of the sacrilege or blasphemy of calling such a place a home.

WHAT A HOME IS.

A home is four walls enclosing one family with identity of interest, and a privacy from outside inspection so complete that it is a world in itself, no one entering except by permission—bolted and barred and chained against all outside inquisitiveness. The phrase so often used in law books and legal circles is mightily suggestive—every man's house is his castle. As much so as though it had drawbridge, portcullis, redoubt, bastion and armed turret. Even the officer of the law may not enter to serve a writ, except the door be voluntarily opened unto him; burglary, or the invasion of it, a crime so offensive that the law clashes its iron jaws on any one who attempts it. Unless it be necessary to stay for longer or shorter time in family hotel or boarding-house—and there are thousands of instances in which it is necessary, as I showed you at the beginning—unless in this exceptional case, let neither wife nor husband consent to such permanent residence.

HAZARDOUS TO MORALS.

The probability is that the wife will have to divide her husband's time with public smoking or reading room, or with some coquettish spider in search of unwary flies; and if you do not entirely lose your husband it will be because he is divinely protected from the disasters that have whelmed thousands of husbands with as good intentions as yours. Neither should the husband, without imperative reason, consent to such a life unless he is sure his wife can withstand the temptation of social dissipation which sweeps across such places with the force of the Atlantic Ocean when driven by a September equinox. Many wives give up their homes for these public residences so that they may give their entire time to operas, theatres, balls, receptions and levees, and they are in a perpetual whirl, like a whip-top, spinning round and round and round very prettily until it loses its equipoise and shoots off into a tangent. But the difference is, in one case it is a top and in the other a soul.

THE LARES AND PENATES.

Beside this there is an assiduous accumulation of little things around the private home which in the aggregate make a great attraction, while the denizen of one of these public residences is apt to say: "What is the use? I have no place to keep them if I should take them." Mementoes, bric-a-brac, curiosities, quaint chair or cosy lounge, upholsteries, pictures, and a thousand things that accrete in a home are discarded or neglected because there is no homestead in which to arrange them. And yet they are the case in which the pearl of domestic happiness is set. You can never become as attached to the appointments of a boarding-house or family hotel as to those things that you can call your own, and are associated with the different members of your household, or with scenes of thrilling import in your domestic history. Blessed is that home in which for a whole lifetime they have been gathering until every figure in the carpet, and every panel of the door, and every casement of the window has a chirography of its own, speaking out something about father or mother, or son or daughter, or friend that was with us a while. What a sacred place it becomes when one can say: "In that room such a one was born; in that bed such a one died; in that chair I sat on the night I heard such a one had received a great public honor; by that stool my child knelt for her last evening prayer; here I sat to greet my son as he came back from a sea voyage; that was father's cane; that was mother's rocking chair." What a joyful and pathetic congress of reminiscences!

HOSPITALITY CURTAILED.

The public residence of hotel and boarding-house abolishes the grace of hospitality. Your guest does not want to come to such a table. No one wants to run such a gauntlet of acute and merciless hyper-criticism. Unless you have a home of your own you will not be able to exercise the best rewarded of all the graces. For exercise of this grace what blessing came to the Shunamite in the restoration of her son to life because she entertained Elisha, and to the widow of Zarephath in the perpetual oil well of the miraculous cruise because she fed a hungry prophet, and to Rahab in the preservation of her life at the demolition of Jericho because she entertained the spies and to Laban in the formation of an interesting family relation because of his entertainment of Jacob, and to Lot in his rescue from the destroyed city because of his entertainment of the angels, and to Mary and Martha and Zaccheus in spiritual blessing because they entertained Christ, and to Publius in the island of Melita in the healing of his father because of the entertainment of Paul drenched from the shipwreck, and of innumerable houses throughout Christendom upon which have come blessings from generation to generation because their doors swung easily open in the enlarging, ennobling, irradiating, and divine grace of hospitality. I do not know what your experience has been, but I have had men and women visiting at my house who left a benediction on every room—in the blessing they asked at the table, in the prayer they offered at the family altar, in the good advice they gave the children, in the gospelization that looked out from every lineament of their countenances; and their departure was the sword of bereavement.

The Queen of Norway, Sweden and Denmark had a royal

CUP OF TEN CURVES,

or lips, each one having on it the name of the distinguished person who had drank from it. And that cup which we offer to others in Christian hospitality, though it be of the plainest earthenware, is a royal cup, and God can read on all its sides the names of those who have taken from it refreshment. But all this is impossible unless you have a home of your own. It is the delusion as to what is necessary for a home that hinders so many from establishing one. Thirty rooms are not necessary, nor twenty, nor fifteen, nor ten, nor five, nor three. In the right way plant a table, and couch, and knife and fork, and a cup, and a chair, and you can raise a young paradise. Just start a home, on however small a scale, and it will grow. When King Cyrus was invited to dine with an humble friend the king made the one condition of his coming that the only dish be one loaf of bread, and the most imperial satisfactions have sometimes banqueted on the plainest fare.

Do not be caught in the delusion of many thousands in postponing a home until they can have an expensive one. That idea is the devil's trap that catches men and women innumerable who will never have any home at all. Capitalists of America, build plain homes for the people. Let this tenement-house system, in which hundreds of thousands of the people of our cities are wallowing in the mire, be broken up by small homes, where people can have their own firesides and their own altar. In this great continent there is room enough for every man and woman to have a home. Morals and civilization and religion demand it.

SMALL HOMES NEEDED

We want done all over this land what George Peabody and Lady Burdett-Coutts did in England, and some of the large manufacturers of this country have done for the villages and cities, in building small houses at cheap rents, so that the middle classes can have separate homes. They are the only class not provided for. The rich have their palaces, and the poor have their poorhouses, and criminals have their jails; but what about the honest middle classes, who are able and willing to work, and yet have small income? Let the capitalists, inspired of God and pure patriotism, rise and build whole streets of small residences. The laborer may have, at the close of the day, to walk or ride further than is desirable to reach it, but when he gets to his destination in the eventide he will find something worthy of being called by that glorious and impassioned and heaven-descended word, "home."

SOMETHING TO SAVE FOR.

Young married man, as soon as you can buy such a place, even if you have to put on it a mortgage reaching from base to cap-stone. The much abused mortgage, which is ruin to a reckless man, to one prudent and provident is the beginning of a competency and a fortune, for the reason he will not be satisfied until he has paid it off, and all the household are put on stringent economies until then. Deny yourself all superfluities and all luxuries until you can say: "Everything in this house is mine, thank God!—every timber, every brick, every foot of plumbing, every door-sill." Do not have your children born in a boarding-house, and do not yourself be buried from one. Have a place where your children can shout and sing and romp without being overhauled for the racket. Have a kitchen where you can do something toward the reformation of evil cookery and the lessening of this nation of dyspeptics. As Napoleon lost one of his great battles by an attack of indigestion, so many men have such

A DAILY WRESTLE

with the food swallowed that they have no strength left for the battle of life; and though your wife may know how to play on all musical instruments, and rival a prima donna, she is not well educated unless she can boil an Irish potato and broil a mutton-chop, since the diet sometimes decides the fate of families and nations.

Have a sitting-room with at least one easy chair, even though you have to take turns at sitting in it, and books out of the public library or of your own purchase for the making of your family intelligent, and checkerboards and guessing matches, with an occasional blind man's buff, which is of all games my favorite. Rouse up your home with all styles of innocent mirth, and gather up in your children's nature a reservoir of exuberance that will pour down refreshing streams when life gets parched, and the dark days come, and the lights go out, and the laughter is smothered into a sob.

CHRIST IN THE HOME.

First, last and all the time, have Christ in your home. Julius Cæsar calmed the fears of an affrighted boatman who was rowing him in a stream by stating: "So long as Cæsar is with you in the same boat no harm can happen." And whatever storm of adversity or bereavement or poverty may strike your home all is well as long as you have Christ the King on board. Make your home so far-reaching in its influence that down to the last moment of your children's life you may hold them with a heavenly charm. At seventy-six years of age the Demosthenes of the American Senate lay dying at Washington—I mean Henry Clay, of Kentucky. His pastor sat at his bedside and the "old man eloquent," after a long and exciting public life, trans-Atlantic and cis-Atlantic, was back again in the scenes of his boyhood, and he kept saying in his dream over and over again: "My mother! mother! mother!" May the parental influence we exert be not only potential but holy, and so the home on earth be the vestibule of our home in heaven, in which place may we all meet—father, mother, son, daughter, brother, sister, grandfather and grandmother, and grandchild, and the entire group of precious ones, of whom we must say in the words of transporting Charles Wesley:

> "One family we dwell in Him,
> One church above, beneath;
> Though now divided by the stream—

> The narrow stream of death;
> One army of the living God,
> To His command we bow;
> Part of the host have crossed the flood,
> And part are crossing now."

EASY DIVORCE.ToC

"What therefore God hath joined together let not man put asunder."—Matthew 19:6

That there are hundreds and thousands of infelicitous homes in America no one will doubt. If there were only one skeleton in the closet, that might be locked up and abandoned; but in many a home there is a skeleton in the hallway and a skeleton in all the apartments.

"UNHAPPILY MARRIED"

are two words descriptive of many a homestead. It needs no orthodox minister to prove to a badly mated pair that there is a hell; they are there now. Sometimes a grand and gracious woman will be thus incarcerated, and her life will be a crucifixion, as was the case with Mrs. Sigourney, the great poetess and the great soul. Sometimes a consecrated man will be united to a fury, as was John Wesley, or united to a vixen, as was John Milton. Sometimes, and generally, both parties are to blame, and Thomas Carlyle is an intolerable scold, and his wife smokes and swears, and Froude, the historian, is mean enough, because of the shekels he gets for the manuscript,[3] to pull aside the curtain from the lifelong squabble at Craigenputtock and Five, Cheyne Row. Some say that for

THE ALLEVIATION

of all these domestic disorders of which we hear, easy divorce is a good prescription. God sometimes authorizes divorce as certainly as He authorizes marriage. I have just as much regard for one lawfully divorced as I have for one lawfully married. But you know and I know that wholesale divorce is one of

OUR NATIONAL SCOURGES.

I am not surprised at this when I think of the influences which have been abroad militating against the marriage relation.

For many years the platforms of the country rang with talk about a free-love millennium. There were meetings of this kind held in the Academy of Music, Brooklyn, Cooper Institute, New York, Tremont Temple, Boston, and all over the land. Some of the women who were most prominent in that movement have since been distinguished for great promiscuosity of affection. Popular themes for such occasions were the tyranny of man, the oppression of the marriage relation, women's rights, and the affinities. Prominent speakers were women with short curls and short dress and very long tongue, everlastingly at war with God because they were created women; while on the platform sat meek men with soft accent and cowed demeanor, apologetic for masculinity, and holding the parasols while the termagant orators went on preaching the gospel of free love.

That campaign of about twenty years set more devils in the marriage relation than will be exorcised in the next fifty. Men and women went home from such meetings so permanently confused as to who were their wives and husbands that they never got out of the perplexity, and the criminal and the civil courts tried to disentangle the Iliad of woes, and this one got alimony, and that one got a limited divorce, and this mother kept the children on condition that the father could sometimes come and look at them, and these went into poorhouses, and those went into an insane asylum, and those went into dissolute public life, and all went to destruction. The mightiest war ever made against the marriage institution was that free-love campaign, sometimes under one name and sometimes under another.

Another influence that has warred upon the marriage relation has been

POLYGAMY IN UTAH.

That is a stereotyped caricature of the marriage relation, and has poisoned the whole land. You might as well think that you can have an arm in a state of mortification and yet the whole body not be sickened, as to have those territories polygamized and yet the body of the nation not feel the putrefaction. Hear it, good men and women of America, that so long ago as 1862 a law was passed by Congress forbidding polygamy in the territories and in all the places where they had jurisdiction. Twenty-two years have passed along and five administrations, armed with all the power of government, and having an army at their disposal, and yet the first brick has not been knocked from that fortress of libertinism.

Every new President in his inaugural has tickled that monster with the straw of condemnation, and every Congress has stultified itself in proposing some plan that would not work. Polygamy stands in Utah and in other of the territories to-day more entrenched, and more brazen, and more puissant, and more braggart, and more infernal, than at any time in its history. James Buchanan, a much-abused man of his day, did more for the extirpation of this villainy than all the subsequent administrations have dared to do. Mr. Buchanan sent out an army, and although it was halted in its work, still he accomplished more than the subsequent administrations, which have done nothing but talk, talk, talk.

I want the people of America to know that for twenty-two years we have had a positive law prohibiting polygamy in the territories. People are crying out for some new law, as though we had not an old law already with which that infamy could be swept into the perdition from which it smoked up. Polygamy in Utah has warred against the marriage relation throughout the land. It is impossible to have such an awful sewer of iniquity sending up its miasma, which is wafted by the winds north, south, east, and west, without the whole land being affected by it.

Another influence that has warred against the marriage relation in this country has been a

PUSTULOUS LITERATURE,

with its millions of sheets every week choked with stories of domestic wrongs, and infidelities, and massacres, and outrages, until it is a wonder to me that there are any decencies or any common-sense left on the subject of marriage. One-half of the news-stands of Brooklyn and New York and all our cities reeking with the filth.

"Now," say some, "we admit all these evils, and the only way to clear them out or correct them is by easy divorce." Well, before we yield to that cry, let us find out

HOW EASY IT IS NOW.

I have looked over the laws of all the States, and I find that while in some States it is easier than in others, in every State it is easy. The State of Illinois through its legislature recites a long list of proper causes for divorce, and then closes up by giving to the courts the right to make a decree of divorce in any case where they deem it expedient. After that you are not surprised at the announcement that in one county of the State of Illinois, in one year, there were 833 divorces. If you want to know how easy it is you have only to look over the records of the States. In Massachusetts 600 divorces in one year; in Maine 478 in one year; in Connecticut 401 divorces in one year; in the city of San Francisco 333 divorces in 1880; in New England in one year 2113 divorces, and in twenty years in New England 20,000. Is that not easy enough?

If the same ratio continue, the ratio of multiplied divorce and multiplied causes of divorce, we are not far from the time when our courts will have to set apart whole days for application, and all you will have to prove against a man will be that he left his slippers in the middle of the floor, and all you will have to prove against a woman will be that her husband's overcoat was buttonless. Causes of divorce doubled in a few years, doubled in France, doubled in England, and doubled in the United States. To show how very easy it is I have to tell you that in Western Reserve, Ohio, the proportion of divorces to marriages celebrated is one to eleven; in Rhode Island is one to thirteen; in Vermont is one to fourteen. Is not that easy enough?

I want you to notice that frequency of divorce always goes along with the dissoluteness of society. Rome for five hundred years had not one case of divorce. Those were her days of glory and virtue. Then the reign of vice began, and divorce became epidemic. If you want to know how rapidly the Empire went down, ask Gibbon. Do you know how the Reign of Terror was introduced in France? By 20,000 cases of divorce in one year in Paris.

WHAT WE WANT

in this country and in all lands is that divorce be made more and more and more difficult. Then people before they enter that relation will be persuaded that there will probably be no escape from it except through the door of the sepulchre. Then they will pause on the verge of that relation until they are fully satisfied that it is best, and that it is right, and that it is happiest. Then we shall have no more marriage in fun. Then men and women will not enter the relation with the idea it is only a trial trip, and if they do not like it they can get out at the first landing. Then this whole question will be taken out of the frivolous into the tremendous, and there will be no more joking about the blossoms in a bride's hair than about the cypress on a coffin.

What we want is that the Congress of the United States at this present session move for the changing the national Constitution so that a law can be passed which shall be uniform all over the country, and what shall be right in one State shall be right in all the States, and what is wrong in one State will be wrong in all the States.

HOW IS IT NOW?

If a party in the marriage relation gets dissatisfied it is only necessary to move to another State to achieve liberation from the domestic tie, and divorce is effected so easy that the first one party knows of it is by seeing it in the newspaper that Rev. Dr. Somebody, on April 14, 1884, introduced into a new marriage relation a member of the household who went off on a pleasure excursion to Newport or a business excursion to Chicago. Married at the bride's house. No cards. There are States of the Union which practically put a premium upon the disintegration of the marriage relation, while there are other States, like our own New York State, that has the pre-eminent idiocy of making marriage lawful at twelve and fourteen years of age.

The Congress of the United States needs to move at the present session for a change of the National Constitution, and then to appoint a committee —not made up of single gentlemen, but of men of families and their families in Washington—who shall prepare a good, honest, righteous, comprehensive,

UNIFORM LAW

that will control everything from Sandy Hook to Golden Horn. That will put an end to brokerages in marriage. That will send divorce lawyers into a decent business. That will set people agitated for many years on the question of how shall they get away from each other to planning how they can adjust themselves to the more or less unfavorable circumstances.

More difficult divorce will put an estoppal to a great extent upon marriage as a financial speculation. There are men who go into the relation just as they go into Wall Street to purchase shares. The female to be invited into the partnership of wedlock is utterly unattractive, and in disposition a suppressed Vesuvius. Everybody knows it, but this masculine candidate for matrimonial orders, through the commercial agency or through the county records, finds out how much estate is to be inherited, and he calculates it. He thinks out how long it will be before the old man will die, and whether he can stand the refractory temper until he does die, and then he enters the relation; for he says, "If I cannot stand it, then through the divorce law I'll back out." That process is going on all the time, and men enter the relation without any moral principle, without any affection, and it is as much a matter of stock speculation as anything that transpired yesterday in Union Pacific, Wabash, and Delaware and Lackawanna.

Now, suppose a man understood, as he ought to understand, that if he goes into that relation there is no possibility of his getting out, or no probability, he would be more slow to put his neck in the yoke. He should say to himself, "Rather than a Caribbean whirlwind with a whole fleet of shipping in its arms, give me a zephyr off fields of sunshine and gardens of peace."

Rigorous divorce law will also hinder women from

THE FATAL MISTAKE

of marrying men to reform them. If a young man by twenty-five years of age or thirty years of age has the habit of strong drink fixed on him, he is as certainly bound for a drunkard's grave as that a train starting out from Grand Central Depot at 8 o'clock to-morrow morning is bound for Albany. The train may not reach Albany, for it may be thrown from the track. The young man may not reach a drunkard's grave, for something may throw him off the iron track of evil habit; but the probability is that the train that starts to-morrow morning at 8 o'clock for Albany will get there and the probability is that the young man who has the habit of strong drink fixed on him before twenty-five or thirty years of age will arrive at a drunkard's grave. She knows he drinks, although he tries to hide it by chewing cloves. Everybody knows he drinks. Parents warn, neighbors and friends warn. She will marry him, she will reform him.

If she is unsuccessful in the experiment, why then the divorce law will emancipate her, because habitual drunkenness is a cause for divorce in Indiana, Kentucky, Florida, Connecticut, and nearly all the States. So the poor thing goes to the altar of sacrifice. If you will show me the poverty-struck streets in any city I will show you the homes of the women who married men to reform them. In one case out of ten thousand it may be a successful experiment. I never saw the successful experiment. But have a rigorous divorce law, and that woman will say, "If I am affianced to that man it is for life; and if now in the ardor of his young love, and I am the prize to be won, he will not give up his cups, when he has won the prize, surely he will not give up his cups." And so that woman will say to the man, "No, sir, you are already married to the club, and you are married to that evil habit, and so you are married twice, and you are a bigamist. Go!"

A rigorous divorce law will also do much to hinder hasty and

INCONSIDERATE MARRIAGES.

Under the impression that one can be easily released people enter the relation without inquiry and without reflection. Romance and impulse rule the day. Perhaps the only ground for the marriage compact is that she likes his looks and he admires the graceful way she passes around the ice cream at the picnic! It is all they know about each other. It is all the preparation for life. A man not able to pay his own board bill, with not a dollar in his possession, will stand at the altar and take the loving hand, and say, "With all my worldly goods I thee endow!" A woman that could not make a loaf of bread to save her life will swear to cherish and obey. A Christian will marry an atheist, and that always makes conjoined wretchedness; for if a man does not believe there is a God, he is neither to be trusted with a dollar nor with your lifelong happiness.

Having read much about love in a cottage people brought up in ease will go and starve in a hovel. Runaway matches and elopements, 999 out of 1000 of which mean death and hell, multiplying on all hands. You see them in every day's newspapers. Our ministers in this region have no defence such as they have in other cities where the banns must be previously published and an officer of the law must give a certificate that all is right; so clergymen are left defenceless, and unite those who ought never to be united. Perhaps they are too young or perhaps they are standing already in some domestic compact.

By the wreck of ten thousand homes, by the holocaust of ten thousand sacrificed men and women, by the hearthstone of the family which is the corner-stone of the State, and in the name of that God who hath set up the family institution and who hath made the breaking of the marital oath the most appalling of all perjuries, I implore the Congress of the United States to make some righteous, uniform law for all the States and from ocean to ocean, on this subject of marriage and divorce.

ADVICE TO LOVERS.

Let me say to the hundreds of young people in this house this morning, before you give your heart and hand in holy alliance, use all caution; inquire outside as to habits, explore the disposition, scrutinize the taste, question the ancestry, and find out the ambitions. Do not take the heroes and the heroines of cheap novels for a model. Do not put your lifetime happiness in the keeping of a man who has a reputation for being a little loose in morals or in the keeping of a woman who dresses fast. Remember that while good looks are a kindly gift of God wrinkles or accident may despoil them. Remember that Byron was no more celebrated for his beauty than for his depravity. Remember that Absalom's hair was not more splendid than his habits were despicable. Hear it, hear it! The only foundation for happy marriage that ever has been or ever will be, is good character.

ASK FATHER AND MOTHER'S COUNSEL

in this most important step of your life. They are good advisers. They are the best friends you ever had. They made more sacrifices for you than any one else ever did, and they will do more to-day for your happiness than any other people. Ask them, and, above all,

ASK GOD.

I used to smile at John Brown of Haddington because when he was about to offer his hand and heart in marriage to one who became his lifelong companion, he opened the conversation by saying, "Let us pray." But I have seen so many shipwrecks on the sea of matrimony, I have made up my mind that John Brown of Haddington was right. A union formed in prayer will be a happy union, though sickness pale the cheek, and poverty empty the bread tray, and death open the small graves, and all the path of life be strewn with thorns, from the marriage altar with its wedding march and orange blossoms clear on down to the last farewell at that gate where Isaac and Rebecca, Abraham and Sarah, Adam and Eve, parted.

And let me say to you who are in this relation, if you make one man or woman happy you have not lived in vain. Christ says that what He is to the Church you ought to be to each other; and if sometimes through difference of opinion or difference of disposition you make up your mind that your marriage was a mistake, patiently bear and forbear, remembering that life at the longest is short and that for those who have been badly mated in this world, death will give quick and immediate bill of divorcement written in letters of green grass on quiet graves. And perhaps, my brother, my sister, perhaps you may appreciate each other better in heaven than you have appreciated each other on earth.

In the "Farm Ballads" our American poet puts into the lips of a repentant husband after a life of married perturbation these suggestive words:

> "And when she dies I wish that she
> would be laid by me,
> And lying together in silence, perhaps
> we will agree.
> And if ever we meet in heaven, I
> would not think it queer
> If we love each other better because
> we quarrelled here."

And let me say to those of you who are in happy married union,

AVOID FIRST QUARRELS;

have no unexplained correspondence with former admirers; cultivate no suspicions; in a moment of bad temper do not rush out and tell the neighbors; do not let any of those gad-abouts of society unload in your house their baggage of gab and tittle-tattle; do not stand on your rights; learn how to apologize; do not be so proud, or so stubborn, or so devilish that you will not make up. Remember that the worst domestic misfortunes and most scandalous divorce cases started from little infelicities. The whole piled-up train of ten rail cars telescoped and smashed at the foot of an embankment one hundred feet down came to that catastrophe by getting two or three inches off the track. Some of the greatest domestic misfortunes and the widest resounding divorce cases have started from little misunderstandings that were allowed to go on and go on until home, and respectability, and religion, and immortal soul went down in the crash, crash!

And, fellow-citizens as well as fellow-Christians, let us have a divine rage against anything that wars on the marriage state. Blessed institution! Instead of two arms to fight the battle of life, four. Instead of two eyes to scrutinize the path of life, four. Instead of two shoulders to lift the burden of life, four. Twice the energy, twice the courage, twice the holy ambition, twice the probability of worldly success, twice the prospects of heaven. Into that matrimonial bower God fetches two souls. Outside the bower room for all contentions, and all bickerings, and all controversies, but inside that bower there is room for only one guest—the angel of love. Let that angel stand at the floral doorway of this Edenic bower with drawn sword to hew down the worst foe of that bower—easy divorce. And for every Paradise lost may there be a Paradise regained. And after we quit our home here may we have a brighter home in heaven at the windows of which this moment are familiar faces watching for our arrival and wondering why so long we tarry.

FOOTNOTES:

[3] Dr. Talmage, in common with many critics, here censures Mr. James Anthony Froude for making the disclosures. It is, however, due to that eminent historian to say that he gives a different explanation of his motives than that suggested by Dr. Talmage of a regard for "shekels." He states that as Mr. Carlyle had selected him as his biographer and given the materials for the work into his hands, he conceived that his duty as a conscientious man was to tell the whole truth. He did it also as a matter of policy as well as of principle. Had he kept back any part, it would have been told with less accuracy by others who knew some of the facts but not all of them.—ED.

MATERNITY.ToC

"Moreover his mother made him a little coat, and brought it to him from year to year, when she came up with her husband to offer the yearly sacrifice."—I SAMUEL 2:19.

The stories of Deborah and Abigail are very apt to discourage a woman's soul. She says within herself: "It is impossible that I ever can achieve any such grandeur of character, and I don't mean to try;" as though a child should refuse to play the eight notes because he cannot execute a "William Tell." This Hannah of the text differs from the persons I just now named. She was an ordinary woman, with ordinary intellectual capacity, placed in the ordinary circumstances, and yet, by extraordinary piety, standing out before all the ages to come.

THE MODEL CHRISTIAN MOTHER.

Hannah was the wife of Elkanah, who was a person very much like herself—unromantic and plain, never having fought a battle or been the subject of a marvelous escape. Neither of them would have been called a genius. Just what you and I might be, that was Elkanah and Hannah. The brightest time in all the history of that family was the birth of Samuel. Although no star ran along the heavens pointing down to his birthplace, I think the angels of God stooped at the coming of so wonderful a prophet.

As Samuel had been given in answer to prayer, Elkanah and all his family, save Hannah, started up to Shiloh to offer sacrifices of thanksgiving. The cradle where the child slept was altar enough for Hannah's grateful heart, but when the boy was old enough she took him to Shiloh and took three bullocks, and an ephah of flour, and a bottle of wine, and made offering of sacrifice unto the Lord, and there, according to a previous vow, she left him; for there he was to stay all the days of his life, and minister in the tabernacle.

Years rolled on, and every year Hannah made with her own hands a garment for Samuel, and took it over to him. The lad would have got along well without that garment, for I suppose he was well clad by the ministry of the temple; but Hannah could not be contented unless she was all the time doing something for her darling boy. "Moreover his mother made him a little coat, and brought it to him from year to year, when she came up with her husband to offer the yearly sacrifice."

I. Hannah stands before you, then, in the first place, as

AN INDUSTRIOUS MOTHER.

There was no need for her to work. Elkanah, her husband, was far from poor. He belonged to a distinguished family; for the Bible tells us that he was the son of Jeroham, the son of Elihu, the son of Tohu, the son of Zuph. "Who were they?" you say. I do not know; but they were distinguished people, no doubt, or their names would not have been mentioned.

Hannah might have seated herself with her family, and, with folded arms and dishevelled hair, read novels from year to year, if there had been any to read; but when I see her making that garment, and taking it over to Samuel, I know she is industrious from principle as well as from pleasure. God would not have a mother become a drudge or a slave; He would have her employ all the helps possible in this day in the rearing of her children. But Hannah ought never to be ashamed to be found making a coat for Samuel.

Most mothers need no counsel in this direction. The wrinkles on their brow, the pallor on their cheek, the thimble-mark on their finger, attest that they are faithful in their maternal duties. The bloom, and the brightness, and the vivacity of girlhood have given place for the grander dignity, and usefulness, and industry of motherhood. But there is

A HEATHENISH IDEA

getting abroad in some of the families of Americans; there are mothers who banish themselves from the home circle. For three fourths of their maternal duties they prove themselves incompetent. They are ignorant of what their children wear, and what their children eat, and what their children read. They intrust to irresponsible persons these young immortals, and allow them to be under influences which may cripple their bodies, or taint their purity, or spoil their manners, or destroy their souls.

From the awkward cut of Samuel's coat you know his mother Hannah did not make it. Out from under flaming chandeliers, and off from imported carpets, and down the granite stairs, there has come a great crowd of children in this day, untrained, saucy, incompetent for all practical duties of life, ready to be caught in the first whirl of crime and sensuality. Indolent and unfaithful mothers will make indolent and unfaithful children. You cannot expect neatness and order in any house where the daughters see nothing but slatternness and upsidedownativeness in their parents. Let Hannah be idle, and most certainly Samuel will grow up idle.

Who are the industrious men in all our occupations and professions? Who are they managing the merchandise of the world, building the walls, tinning the roofs, weaving the carpets, making the laws, governing the nations, making the earth to quake, and heave, and roar, and rattle with the tread of gigantic enterprises? Who are they? For the most part they descended from industrious mothers, who, in the old homestead, used to spin their own yarn, and weave their own carpets, and plait their own doormats, and flag their own chairs, and do their own work. The stalwart men and the

INFLUENTIAL WOMEN

of this day, ninety-nine out of a hundred of them, came from such an illustrious ancestry of hard knuckles and homespun.

And who are these people in society, light as froth, blown every whither of temptation and fashion—the peddlers of filthy stories, the dancing-jacks of political parties, the scum of society, the tavern-lounging, the store-infesting, the men of low wink, and filthy chuckle, and brass breast-pins, and rotten associations? For the most part, they came from mothers idle and disgusting—the scandal-mongers of society, going from house to house, attending to everybody's business but their own, believing in witches, and ghosts, and horseshoes to keep the devil out of the churn, and by a godless life setting their children on the very verge of hell. The mothers of Samuel Johnson, and of Alfred the Great, and Isaac Newton, and of St. Augustine, and of Richard Cecil, and of President Edwards, for the most part were industrious, hard-working mothers.

Now, while I congratulate all Christian mothers upon the wealth and the modern science which may afford them all kinds of help, let me say that every mother ought to be observant of her children's walk, her children's behavior, her children's food, her children's looks, her children's companionships. However much help Hannah may have, I think she ought every year, at least, make one garment for Samuel. The Lord have mercy on the man who is so unfortunate as to have had a lazy mother!

II. Again, Hannah stands before you as

AN INTELLIGENT MOTHER.

From the way in which she talked in this chapter, and from the way she managed this boy, you know she was intelligent. There are no persons in the community who need to be so wise and well-informed as mothers.

Oh, this work of culture in children for this world and the next! This child is timid, and it must be roused up and pushed out into activity. This child is forward, and he must be held back and tamed down into modesty and politeness. Rewards for one, punishments for another. That which will make George will ruin John. The rod is necessary in one case, while a frown of displeasure is more than enough in another. Whipping and a dark closet do not exhaust all the rounds of domestic discipline. There have been children who have grown up and gone to glory without ever having had their ears boxed.

Oh, how much care and intelligence are necessary in the rearing of children! But in this day, when there are so many books on the subject, no parent is excusable in being ignorant of the best mode of

BRINGING UP A CHILD.

If parents knew more of dietetics there would not be so many dyspeptic stomachs and weak nerves and inactive livers among children. If parents knew more of physiology there would not be so many curved spines and cramped chests and inflamed throats and diseased lungs as there are among children. If parents knew more of art, and were in sympathy with all that is beautiful, there would not be so many children coming out in the world with boorish proclivities. If parents knew more of Christ, and practised more of His religion, there would not be so many little feet already starting on the wrong road, and all around us voices of riot and blasphemy would not come up with such ecstasy of infernal triumph.

The eaglets in the eyrie have no advantages over the eaglets of a thousand years ago; the kids have no superior way of climbing up the rocks than the old goats taught hundreds of years ago; the whelps know no more now than did the whelps of ages ago—they are taught no more by the lions of the desert; but it is a shame that in this day, when there are so many opportunities of improving ourselves in the best manner of cultivating children, that so often there is no more advancement in this respect than there has been among the kids and the eaglets and the whelps.

III. Again, Hannah stands before you as

A CHRISTIAN MOTHER.

From her prayers and from the way she consecrated her boy to God, I know that she was good. A mother may have the finest culture, the most brilliant surroundings; but she is not fit for her duties unless she be a Christian mother. There may be well-read libraries in the house, and exquisite music in the parlor, and the canvases of the best artists adorning the walls, and the wardrobe be crowded with tasteful apparel, and the children be wonderful for their attainments, and make the house ring with laughter and innocent mirth, but there is something woeful-looking in that house if it be not also the residence of a Christian mother.

I bless God that there are not many prayerless mothers—not many of them. The weight of the responsibility is so great that they feel the need of a divine hand to help, and a divine voice to comfort and a divine heart to sympathize. Thousands of mothers have been led into the kingdom of God by the hands of their little children. There were hundreds of mothers who would not have been Christians had it not been for the prattle of their little ones. Standing some day in the nursery, they bethought themselves: "This child God has given me to raise for eternity. What is my influence upon it? Not being a Christian myself, how can I ever expect him to become a Christian? Lord, help me!" Are there

ANXIOUS MOTHERS

who know nothing of the infinite help of religion? Then I commend to them Hannah, the pious mother of Samuel. Do not think it is absolutely impossible that your children may come up iniquitous. Out of just such fair brows and bright eyes, and soft hands, and innocent hearts, crime gets its victims—extirpating purity from the heart, and rubbing out the smoothness from the brow, and quenching the lustre of the eye, and shriveling up and poisoning and putrefying and scathing and scalding and blasting and burning with shame and woe.

Every child is a bundle of tremendous possibilities; and whether that child shall come forth to life, its heart attuned to the eternal harmonies, and, after a life of usefulness on earth, go to a life of joy in heaven; or whether across it shall jar eternal discords, and, after a life of wrong-doing on earth, it shall go to a home of impenetrable darkness and an abyss of immeasurable plunge, is being decided by nursery song and Sabbath lesson and evening prayer and walk and ride and look and frown and smile. Oh, how many children in glory, crowding all the battlements, and lifting a million-voiced hosanna, brought to God through Christian parentage!

One hundred and twenty clergymen were together, and they were telling their experience and their ancestry; and of the one hundred and twenty clergymen, how many of them, do you suppose, assigned as the means of their conversion the influence of a Christian mother? One hundred out of the one hundred and twenty! Philip Doddridge was brought to God by the Scripture lesson on the Dutch tiles of a chimney fireplace. The mother thinks she is only rocking a child, but at the same time she may be rocking the fate of nations, rocking the glories of heaven. The same maternal power that may lift the child up may press a child down.

A daughter came to

A WORLDLY MOTHER

and said she was anxious about her sins, and she had been praying all night. The mother said: "Oh, stop praying! I don't believe in praying. Get over all these religious notions and I'll give you a dress that will cost $500, and you may wear it next week to that party." The daughter took the dress, and she moved in the gay circle the gayest of all the gay, that night; and sure enough all the religious impressions were gone and she stopped praying. A few months after she came to die, and in her closing moments said: "Mother, I wish you would bring me that dress that cost $500." The mother thought it a very strange request, but she brought it to please the dying child. "Now," said the daughter, "mother, hang that dress on the foot of my bed," and the dress was hung there, on the foot of the bed. Then the dying girl got up on one elbow and looked at her mother, and then pointed to the dress, and said: "Mother, that dress is the price of my soul." Oh, what a momentous thing it is to be a mother!

IV. Again, and lastly, Hannah stands before you

THE REWARDED MOTHER.

For all the coats she made for Samuel, for all the prayers she offered for him, for the discipline exerted over him she got abundant compensation in the piety and the usefulness and the popularity of her son Samuel; and that is true in all ages. Every mother gets full pay for all the prayers and tears in behalf of her children. That man useful in commercial life; that man prominent in a profession; that master mechanic—why, every step he takes in life has an echo of gladness in the old heart that long ago taught him to be a Christian, and heroic and earnest.

The story of what you have done, or what you have written, of the influence you exerted, has gone back to the old homestead—for there is some one always ready to carry good tidings—and that story makes the needle in the old mother's tremulous hand fly quicker, and the flail in the father's hand come down on the barn floor with a vigorous thump. Parents love to hear good news from their children. Do you send them good news always?

Look out for the young man who speaks of his father as "the governor," the "squire," or the "old chap." Look out for the young woman who calls her mother her "maternal ancestor," or the "old woman." "The eye that mocketh at his father, and refuseth to obey his mother, the ravens of the valley shall pick it out, and the young eagles shall eat it."

God grant that all these parents may have the great satisfaction of seeing their children grow up Christians. But, oh! the pang of that mother, who, after a life of street gadding and gossip retailing, hanging on the children the fripperies and follies of this world, sees those children tossed out on the sea of life like foam on the wave, or nonentities in a world where only bravery and stalwart character can stand the shock! But blessed be the mother who looks upon her children as sons and daughters of the Lord Almighty.

Oh! the satisfaction of Hannah in seeing Samuel serving at the altar; of Mother Eunice in seeing her Timothy learned in the Scriptures. That is the mother's recompense, to see children coming up useful in the world, reclaiming the lost, healing the sick, pitying the ignorant, earnest and useful in every sphere. That throws a new light back on the old family Bible whenever she reads it, and that will be ointment to soothe the aching limbs of decrepitude, and light up the closing hours of life's day with the glories of an autumnal sunset!

There she sits,

THE OLD CHRISTIAN MOTHER,

ripe for heaven. Her eyesight is almost gone, but the splendors of the celestial city kindle up her vision. The gray light of heaven's morn has struck through the gray locks which are folded back over the wrinkled temples. She stoops very much now under the burden of care she used to carry for her children. She sits at home, too old to find her way to the house of God; but while she sits there, all the past comes back, and the children that forty years ago tripped around her armchair with their griefs and joys and sorrows—those children are gone now. Some caught up into a better realm, where they shall never die, and others out in the broad world, testing the excellency of a Christian mother's discipline. Her last days are full of peace; and calmer and sweeter will her spirit become, until the gates of life shall lift and let in the worn-out pilgrim into eternal springtide and youth, where the limbs never ache, and the eyes never grow dim, and the staff of the exhausted and decrepit pilgrim shall become the palm of the immortal athlete!

THE CHILDREN'S PATRIMONY.ToC

"Whose son art thou, thou young man?"—Samuel 17:58.

Never was there a more unequal fight than that between David and Goliath. David five feet high; Goliath ten. David a shepherd boy, brought up amid rural scenes; Goliath a warrior by profession. Goliath a mountain of braggadocia; David a marvel of humility. Goliath armed with an iron spear; David armed with a sling with smooth stones from the brook. But you are not to despise these latter weapons. There was a regiment of slingers in the Assyrian army and a regiment of slingers in the Egyptian army, and they made terrible execution, and they could cast a stone with as much precision and force as now can be hurled shot or shell. The Greeks in their army had slingers who would throw leaden plummets inscribed with the irritating words: "Take this!" So it was a mighty weapon David employed in that famous combat.

A Jewish rabbi says that the probability is that Goliath was in such contempt for David, that in a paroxysm of laughter he threw his head back, and his helmet fell off, and David saw the uncovered forehead, and his opportunity had come, and taking his sling and swinging it around his head two or three times, and aiming at that uncovered forehead, he crushed it in like an egg-shell. The battle over,

BEHOLD A TABLEAU:

King Saul sitting, little David standing, his fingers clutched into the hair of decapitated Goliath. As Saul sees David standing there holding in his hand the ghastly, reeking, staring trophy, evidence of the complete victory over God's enemies, the king wonders what parentage was honored by such heroism, and in my text he asks David his pedigree: "Whose son art thou, thou young man?"

The king saw what you and I see, that this question of heredity is a mighty question. The longer I live the more

I BELIEVE IN BLOOD

—good blood, bad blood, proud blood, humble blood, honest blood, thieving blood, heroic blood, cowardly blood. The tendency may skip a generation or two, but it is sure to come out, as in a little child you sometimes see a similarity to a great-grandfather whose picture hangs on the wall. That the physical and mental and moral qualities are inheritable is patent to any one who keeps his eyes open. The similarity is so striking sometimes as to be amusing. Great families, regal or literary, are apt to have the characteristics all down through the generations, and what is more perceptible in such families may be seen on a smaller scale in all families. A thousand years have no power to obliterate the difference.

ROYAL RASCALS.

The large lip of the House of Austria is seen in all the generations, and is called the Hapsburg lip. The House of Stuart always means in all generations cruelty and bigotry and sensuality. Witness Queen of Scotts. Witness Charles I. and Charles II. Witness James I. and James II. and all the other scoundrels of that imperial line.

Scottish blood means persistence, English blood means reverence for the ancient, Welsh blood means religiosity, Danish blood means fondness for the sea, Indian blood means roaming disposition, Celtic blood means fervidity, Roman blood means conquest.

The Jewish facility for accumulation you may trace clear back to Abraham, of whom the Bible says "he was rich in silver and gold and cattle," and to Isaac and Jacob, who had the same

FAMILY CHARACTERISTICS.

Some families are characterized by longevity, and they have a tenacity of life positively Methuselahish. Others are characterized by Goliathian stature, and you can see it for one generation, two generations, five generations, in all the generations. Vigorous theology runs on in the line of the Alexanders. Tragedy runs on in the family of the Kembles. Literature runs on in the line of the Trollopes. Philanthropy runs on in the line of the Wilberforces. Statesmanship runs on in the line of the Adamses. Henry and Catharine of Navarre religious, all their families religious. The celebrated family of the Casini, all mathematicians. The celebrated family of the Medici—grandfather, son and Catharine—all remarkable for keen intellect. The celebrated family of Gustavus Adolphus, all warriors.

This law of heredity asserts itself without reference to social or political condition, for you sometimes find the ignoble in high place and the honorable in obscure place. A descendant of Edward I. a toll gatherer. A descendant of Edward III. a door-keeper. A descendant of the Duke of Northumberland a trunk-maker. Some of the mightiest families of England are extinct, while some of those most honored in the peerage go back to an ancestry of hard knuckles and rough exterior. This law of heredity entirely independent of social or political condition.

Then you find avarice and jealousy and sensuality and fraud having full swing in some families. The violent temper of Frederick William is the inheritance of Frederick the Great. It is not a theory to be set forth by worldly philosophy only, but by divine authority. Do you not remember how the Bible speaks of "a chosen generation," of "the generation of the righteous," of "the generation of vipers," of an "untoward generation," of "a stubborn generation," of "the iniquity of the past visited upon the children unto the third and fourth generation?" So that the text comes to-day with the force of a projectile hurled from mightiest catapult: "Whose son art thou, thou young man?"

"Well," says some one, "that theory discharges me from all responsibility. Born of sanctified parents we are bound to be good and we cannot help ourselves. Born of unrighteous parentage we are bound to be evil and we cannot help ourselves."

TWO INACCURACIES.

As much as if you should say, "The centripetal force in nature has a tendency to bring everything to the centre, and therefore all things come to the centre. The centrifugal force in nature has a tendency to throw out everything to the periphery, and therefore everything will go out to the periphery." You know as well as I know that you can make the centripetal overcome the centrifugal, and you can make the centrifugal overcome the centripetal. As when there is a mighty tide of good in a family that may be overcome by determination to evil, as in the case of Aaron Burr, the libertine, who had for father President Burr, the consecrated; as in the case of Pierrepont Edwards, the scourge of New York society seventy years ago, who had a Christian ancestry; while on the other hand some of the best men and women of this day are those who have come of an ancestry of which it would not be courteous to speak in their presence.

YOUR DUTY.

The practical and useful object of this sermon is to show to you that if you have come of a Christian ancestry, then you are solemnly bound to preserve and develop the glorious inheritance; or if you have come of a depraved ancestry, then it is your duty to brace yourself against the evil tendency by all prayer and Christian determination, and you are to find out what are the family frailties, and in arming the castle put the strongest guard at the weakest gate. With these smooth stones from the brook I hope to strike you, not where David struck Goliath, in the head, but where Nathan struck David, in the heart. "Whose son art thou, thou young man?"

There is something in the periodical holidays to bring up

THE OLD FOLKS.

Sometime in the winter holiday, when we are accustomed to gather our families together, old times have come back again, and our thoughts have been set to the tune of "Auld Lang Syne." The old folks were so busy at such times in making us happy, and perhaps on less resource made their sons and daughters happier than you on larger resource are able to make your sons and daughters happy. The snow lay two feet above their graves, but they shook off the white blankets and mingled in the holiday festivities —the same wrinkles, the same stoop of shoulder under the weight of age, the same old style of dress or coat, the same smile, the same tones of voice. I hope you remember them before they went away. If not, I hope there are those who have recited to you what they were, and that there may be in your house some article of dress or furniture with which you associate their memories. I want to arouse the most sacred memories of your heart while I make the impassioned interrogatory in regard to your pedigree: "Whose son art thou, thou young man?"

I. First, I accost all those who are descended of a

CHRISTIAN ANCESTRY.

I do not ask if your parents were perfect. There are no perfect people now, and I do not suppose there were any perfect people then. Perhaps there was sometimes too much blood in their eye when they chastised you. But from what I know of you, you got no more than you deserved, and perhaps a little more chastisement would have been salutary. But you are willing to acknowledge, I think, that they wanted to do right. From what you overheard in conversations, and from what you saw at the family altar and at neighborhood obsequies, you know that they had invited God into their heart and life. There was something that sustained those old people supernaturally. You have no doubt about their destiny. You expect if you ever get to heaven to meet them as certainly as you expect to meet the Lord Jesus Christ.

That early association has been a charm for you. There was a time when you got right up from a house of iniquity and walked out into the fresh air because you thought your mother was looking at you. You have never been very happy in sin because of a sweet old face that would present itself. Tremulous voices from the past accosted you until they were seemingly audible, and you looked around to see who spoke. There was an estate not mentioned in the last will and testament, a vast estate of prayer and holy example and Christian entreaty and glorious memory. The survivors of the family gathered to hear the will read, and this was to be kept, and that was to be sold, and it was share and share alike. But there was

AN UNWRITTEN WILL

that read something like this: "In the name of God, Amen. I, being of sound mind, bequeath to my children all my prayers for their salvation; I bequeath to them all the results of a lifetime's toil; I bequeath to them the Christian religion which has been so much comfort to me, and I hope may be solace for them; I bequeath to them a hope of reunion when the partings of life are over; share and share alike may they have in eternal riches. I bequeath to them the wish that they may avoid my errors and copy anything that may have been worthy. In the name of the God who made me, and the Christ who redeemed me, and the Holy Ghost who sanctifies me, I make this my last will and testament. Witness, all ye hosts of heaven. Witness, time, witness, eternity. Signed, sealed, and delivered in this our dying hour. Father and Mother."

You did not get that will proved at the surrogate's office; but I take it out to-day and I read it to you; I take it out of the alcoves of your heart; I shake the dust off it, I ask you will you accept that inheritance, or will you break the will? O ye of Christian ancestry, you have a responsibility vast beyond all measurement! God will not let you off with just being as good as ordinary people when you had such extraordinary advantage. Ought not a flower planted in a hot-house be more thrifty than a flower planted outside in the storm? Ought not a factory turned by the Housatonic do more work than a factory turned by a thin and shallow mountain stream? Ought not you of great early opportunity be better than those who had a cradle unblessed?

THE CAPITAL ACCOUNT.

A father sets his son up in business. He keeps an account of all the expenditures. So much for store fixtures, so much for rent, so much for this, so much for that, and all the items aggregated, and the father expects the son to give an account. Your heavenly Father charges against you all the advantages of a pious ancestry—so many prayers, so much Christian example, so many kind entreaties—all these gracious influences one tremendous aggregate, and He asks you for an account of it.

Ought not you to be better than those who had no such advantages? Better have been a foundling picked up off the city commons than with such magnificent inheritance of consecration to turn out indifferently.

Ought not you, my brother, to be better, having had Christian nurture, than that man who can truly say this morning: "The first word I remember my father speaking to me was an oath; the first time I remember my father taking hold of me was in wrath; I never saw a Bible till I was ten years of age, and then I was told it was a pack of lies. The first twenty years of my life I was associated with the vicious. I seemed to be walled in by sin and death." Now, my brother, ought you not—I leave it as a matter of fairness with you—ought you not to be far better than those who had no early Christian influence?

Standing as you do between the generation that is past and the generation that is to come, are you going to pass the blessing on, or are you going to have your life the gulf in which that tide of blessing shall drop out of sight forever? You are

THE TRUSTEE OF PIETY

in that ancestral line, and are you going to augment or squander that solemn trust fund? are you going to disinherit your sons and daughters of the heirloom which your parents left you? Ah! that cannot be possible, that cannot be possible that you are going to take such a position as that. You are very careful about the life insurances, and careful about the deeds, and careful about the mortgages, and careful about the title of your property, because when you step off the stage you want your children to get it all. Are you making no provision that they shall get grandfather and grandmother's religion? Oh, what a last will and testament you are making, my brother! "In the name of God, Amen. I, being of sound mind, make this my last will and testament. I bequeath to my children all the money I ever made and all the houses I own; but I disinherit them, I rob them of the ancestral grace and the Christian influence that I inherited. I have squandered that on my own worldliness. Share and share alike must they in the misfortune and the everlasting outrage. Signed, sealed and delivered in the presence of God and men and angels and devils and all the generations of earth and heaven and hell, March, 1886."

O ye of highly favored ancestry, wake up this morning to a sense of your opportunity and your responsibility. I think there must be

AN OLD CRADLE,

or a fragment of a cradle somewhere that could tell a story of midnight supplication in your behalf. Where is the old rocking-chair in which you were sung to sleep with the holy nursery rhyme? Where is the old clock that ticked away the moments of that sickness on that awful night when there were but three of you awake—you and God and mother? Is there not an old staff in some closet? is there not an old family Bible on some shelf that seems to address you, saying: "My son, my daughter, how can you reject that God who so kindly dealt with us all our lives and to whom we commended you in our prayers living and dying? By the memory of the old homestead, by the family altar, by our dying pillow, by the graves in which our bodies sleep while our spirits hover, we beg you to turn over a new leaf for the new year." Oh, the power of ancestral piety, well illustrated by a young man of New York who attended a prayer-meeting one night and asked for prayer, and then went home and wrote down these words:

AN ENTRY IN A DIARY.

"Twenty-five years ago to-night my mother went to heaven, my beautiful, blessed mother, and I have been alone, tossed up and down upon the billows of life's tempestuous ocean. Shall I ever go to heaven? She told me I must meet her in heaven. When she took her boy's hand in hers and turned her gentle, loving eyes on me, and gazed earnestly and long into my face, and then lifted them to heaven in that last prayer, she prayed that I might meet her in heaven. I wonder if I ever shall.

"My mother's prayers! Oh, my sweet, blessed mother's prayers! Did ever boy have such a mother as I had? For twenty-five years I have not heard her pray until to-night. I have heard all her prayers over again. They have had, in fact, a terrible resurrection. Oh, how she was wont to pray! She prayed as they prayed to-night, so earnest, so importunate, so believing. Shall I ever be a Christian? She was a Christian. Oh, how bright and pure and happy was her life! She was a cheerful and happy Christian. There is

"MY MOTHER'S BIBLE.

"I have not opened it for years. Did she believe I could ever neglect her precious Bible? She surely thought I would read it much and often. How often has she read it to me. Blessed mother, did you pray in vain for your boy? It shall not be in vain. Ah! no, no, it shall not be in vain. I will pray for myself. Who has sinned against so much instruction as I have? against so many precious prayers put up to heaven for me by one of the most lovely, tender, pious, confiding, trusting of mothers in her heavenly Father's care and grace? She never doubted. She believed. She always prayed as if she did. My Bible, my mother's Bible and my conscience teach what I am and what I have made myself. Oh, the bitter pangs of an accusing conscience! I need a Saviour mighty to save. I must seek Him. I will. I am on the sea of existence, and I can never get off from it. I am afloat. No anchor, no rudder, no compass, no book of instructions, for I have put them all away from me. Saviour of the perishing, save or I perish."

Do you wonder that the next day he arose in a prayer-meeting and said: "My brethren, I stand before you a monument of God's amazing mercy and goodness, forever blessed be His holy name; all I have and all I am I consecrate to Jesus, my Saviour and my God?" Oh, the power of ancestral prayer. Hear it! Hear it!

II. But I turn for a moment to those who had

EVIL PARENTAGE,

and I want to tell you that the highest thrones in heaven and the mightiest triumphs and the brightest crowns will be for those who had evil parentage, but who by the grace of God conquered. As useful, as splendid a gentleman as I know of to-day had for father a man who died blaspheming God until the neighbors had to put their fingers in their ears to shut out the horror. One of the most consecrated and useful Christian ministers of to-day was born of a drunken horse-jockey. Tide of evil tremendous in some families. It is like Niagara Rapids, and yet men have clung to a rock and been rescued.

There is a family in New York whose wealth has rolled up into many millions that was founded by a man who, after he had vast estate sent back a paper of tacks because they were two cents more than he expected. Grip and grind and gouge in the fourth generation—I suppose it will be grip and grind and gouge in the twentieth generation. The thirst for intoxicants has burned down through the arteries of a hundred and fifty years. Pugnacity or combativeness characterize other families. Sometimes one form of evil, sometimes another form of evil. But

IT MAY BE RESISTED,

it has been resisted. If the family frailty be avarice, cultivate unselfishness and charity, and teach your children never to eat an apple without offering somebody else half of it. Is the family frailty combativeness, keep out of the company of quick-tempered people, and never answer an impertinent question until you have counted a hundred both ways, and after you have written an angry letter keep it a week before you send it, and then burn it up! Is the family frailty timidity and cowardice, cultivate backbone, read the biography of brave men like Joshua or Paul, and see if you cannot get a little iron in your blood. Find out what the family frailty is, and set body, mind and soul in battle array.

CONQUER YOUR WILL.

I think the genealogical table was put in the first chapter of the New Testament, not only to show our Lord's pedigree, but to show that a man may rise up in an ancestral line and beat back successfully all the influences of bad heredity. See in that genealogical table that good King Asa came of vile King Abia. See in that genealogical table that Joseph and Mary and the most illustrious Being that ever touched our world, or ever will touch it, had in their ancestral line scandalous Rehoboam and Tamar and Bathsheba. If this world is ever to be Edenized—and it will be—all the infected families of the earth are to be regenerated, and there will some one arise in each family line and open a new genealogical table. There will be some Joseph in the line to reverse the evil influence of Rehoboam, and there will be some Mary in the line to reverse the evil influence of Bathsheba. Perhaps the star of hope may point down to your manger. Perhaps you are to be the hero or the heroine that is to put down the brakes and stop that long train of genealogical tendencies and switch it off on another track from that on which it has been running for a century. You do that, and I will promise you as fine a palace as the architects of heaven can build, the archway inscribed with the words: "More than conqueror."

ADOPTED CHILDREN.

But whatever your heredity, let me say, you may be sons and daughters of the Lord God Almighty. Estranged children from the homestead come back through the open gate of adoption. There is royal blood in our veins. There are crowns in our escutcheon. Our Father is King. Our Brother is King. We may be kings and queens unto God forever. Come and sit down on the ivory bench of the palace. Come and wash in the fountains that fall into the basins of crystal and alabaster. Come and look out of the upholstered window upon gardens of azalea and amaranth. Hear the full burst of the orchestra while you banquet with potentates and victors. Oh, when the text sweeps backward, let it not stop at the cradle that rocked your infancy, but at the cradle that rocked the first world, and when the text sweeps forward, let it not stop at your grave, but at the throne on which you may reign forever and ever! "Whose son art thou, thou young man?" Son of God! Heir of mortality! Take your inheritance!

THE MOTHER OF ALL.ToC

"And the Lord God caused a deep sleep to fall upon Adam, and he slept; and He took one of his ribs, and closed up the flesh instead thereof; and the rib, which the Lord God had taken from man, made He a woman, and brought her unto the man."—GENESIS 2:21, 22.

It is the first Saturday afternoon in the world's existence. Ever since sunrise Adam has been watching the brilliant pageantry of wings and scales and clouds, and in his first lessons in zoology and ornithology and ichthyology he has noticed that the robins fly the air in twos, and that the fish swim the water in twos, and that the lions walk the fields in twos, and in the warm redolence of that Saturday afternoon he falls off into slumber; and as if by allegory to teach all ages that the greatest of earthly blessings is sound sleep, this paradisaical somnolence ends with the discovery on the part of Adam of

A CORRESPONDING INTELLIGENCE

just landed on the new planet. Of the mother of all the living I speak—Eve, the first, the fairest and the best.

I make me a garden. I inlay the paths with mountain moss, and I border them with pearls from Ceylon and diamonds from Golconda. Here and there are fountains tossing in the sunlight, and ponds that ripple under the paddling of the swans. I gather me lilies from the Amazon, and orange groves from the tropics, and tamarinds from Goyaz. There are woodbine and honey-suckle climbing over the wall, and starred spaniels sprawling themselves on the grass. I invite amid these trees the larks, and the brown thrushes, and the robins, and all the brightest birds of heaven, and they stir the air with infinite chirp and carol. And yet the place is a desert filled with darkness and death as compared with

THE RESIDENCE OF THE WOMAN

of the text, the subject of my morning story. Never since have such skies looked down through such leaves into such waters! Never has river wave had such curve and sheen and bank as adorned the Pison, the Havilah, the Gihon, and the Hiddakel, even the pebbles being bdellium and onyx stone! What fruits, with no curculio to sting the rind! What flowers, with no slug to gnaw the root! What atmosphere, with no frost to chill and with no heat to consume! Bright colors tangled in the grass. Perfume in the air. Music in the sky. Bird's warble and tree's hum, and waterfall's dash. Great scene of gladness and love and joy.

Right there under a bower of leaf and vine and shrub occurred

THE FIRST MARRIAGE.

Adam took the hand of this immaculate daughter of God and pronounced the ceremony when he said: "Bone of my bone, and flesh of my flesh."

A FORBIDDEN TREE

stood in the midst of that exquisite park. Eve sauntering out one day alone looks up at the tree and sees the beautiful fruit, and wonders if it is sweet, and wonders if it is sour, and standing there, says: "I think I will just put my hand upon the fruit; it will do no damage to the tree; I will not take the fruit to eat, but I will just take it down to examine it." She examined the fruit. She said: "I do not think there can be any harm in my just breaking the rind of it." She put the fruit to her teeth, she tasted, she invited Adam also to taste of the fruit, the door of the world opened, and the monster Sin entered. Let the heavens gather blackness, and the winds sigh on the bosom of the hills, and cavern and desert and earth and sky join in one long, deep, hell-rending howl:

"THE WORLD IS LOST!"

Beasts that before were harmless and full of play put forth claw, and sting, and tooth, and tusk. Birds whet their beak for prey. Clouds troop in the sky. Sharp thorns shoot up through the soft grass. Blastings on the leaves. All the chords of that great harmony are snapped. Upon the brightest home this world ever saw our first parents turned their back and led forth on a path of sorrow the broken-hearted myriads of a ruined race.

Do you not see, in the first place, the danger of a poorly regulated

INQUISITIVENESS?

She wanted to know how the fruit tasted. She found out, but six thousand years have deplored that unhealthful curiosity. Healthy curiosity has done a great deal for letters, for art, for science and for religion. It has gone down into the depths of the earth with the geologist and seen the first chapter of Genesis written in the book of nature illustrated with engraving on rock, and it stood with the antiquarian while he blew the trumpet of resurrection over buried Herculaneum and Pompeii, until from their sepulchre there came up shaft and terrace and amphitheatre. Healthful curiosity has enlarged the telescopic vision of the astronomer until worlds hidden in the distant heavens have trooped forth and have joined the choir praising the

Lord. Planet weighed against planet and wildest comet lassoed with resplendent law.

HEALTHFUL CURIOSITY

has gone down and found the tracks of the eternal God in the polypi and the starfish under the sea and the majesty of the great Jehovah encamped under the gorgeous curtains of the dahlia. It has studied the spots on the sun, and the larvæ in a beech leaf, and the light under fire-fly's wing, and the terrible eye glance of a condor pitching from Chimborazo. It has studied the myriads of animalculæ that make up the phosphorescence in a ship's wake, and the mighty maze of suns, and spheres, and constellations, and galaxies that blaze on in the march of God. Healthful curiosity has stood by the inventor until forces that were hidden for ages came to wheels, and levers, and shafts, and shuttles—forces that fly the air, or swim the sea, or cleave the mountain until the earth jars, and roars, and rings, and crackles, and booms, with strange mechanism, and ships with nostrils of hot steam and yokes of fire draw the continents together.

I say nothing against healthful curiosity. May it have other Leyden jars, and other electric batteries, and other voltaic piles, and other magnifying glasses with which to storm the barred castles of the natural world until it shall surrender its last secret. We thank God for the geological curiosity of Professor Hitchcock, and the mechanical curiosity of Liebig, and the zoölogical curiosity of Cuvier, and the inventive curiosity of Edison; but we must admit that unhealthful and irregular inquisitiveness has rushed thousands and tens of thousands into ruin.

Eve just tasted the fruit. She was curious to find out how it tasted, and that

CURIOSITY BLASTED HER

and blasted all nations. So there are clergy in this day inspired by unhealthful inquisitiveness who have tried to look through the keyhole of God's mysteries, mysteries that were barred and bolted from all human inspection, and they have wrenched their whole moral nature out of joint by trying to pluck fruit from branches beyond their reach, or have come out on limbs of the tree from which they have tumbled into ruin without remedy. A thousand trees of religious knowledge from which we may eat and get advantage; but from certain

TREES OF MYSTERY

how many have plucked their ruin! Election, free agency, trinity, resurrection—in the discussion of these subjects hundreds and thousands of people ruin the soul. There are men who have actually been kept out of the kingdom of heaven because they could not understand who Melchisedec was not!

Oh, how many have been destroyed by an unhealthful inquisitiveness! It is seen in all directions. There are those who stand with the eye-stare and mouth-gape of curiosity. They are the first to hear a falsehood, build it another story high and two wings to it. About other people's apparel, about other people's business, about other people's financial condition, about other people's affairs, they are over anxious. Every nice piece of gossip stops at their door, and they fatten and luxuriate in the endless round of the great world of tittle-tattle. They invite and sumptuously entertain at their house Colonel Twaddle and Esquire Chitchat and Governor Smalltalk. Whoever hath an innuendo, whoever hath a scandal, whoever hath a valuable secret, let him come and sacrifice it to

THIS GODDESS OF SPLUTTER.

Thousands of Adams and Eves do nothing but eat fruit that does not belong to them. Men quite well known as mathematicians failing in this computation of moral algebra: good sense plus good breeding, minus curiosity, equals minding your own affairs!

Then, how many young men through curiosity go through the whole realm of

FRENCH NOVELS,

to see whether they are really as bad as moralists have pronounced them! They come near the verge of the precipice just to look off. They want to see how far it really is down, but they lose their balance while they look, and fall into remediless ruin; or, catching themselves, clamber up, bleeding and ghastly, on the rock, gibbering with curses or groaning ineffectual prayer. By all means encourage healthful inquisitiveness, by all means discourage ill regulated curiosity.

TREACHEROUS FRUIT.

The subject of the morning also impresses me with the fact that fruits that are sweet to the taste may afterward produce great agony. Forbidden fruit for Eve was so pleasant she invited her husband also to take of it; but her banishment from Paradise, and six thousand years of sorrow, and wretchedness, and war, and woe paid for that luxury. Sin may be very sweet at the start, and it may induce great wretchedness afterward. The cup of sin is sparkling at the top, but there is death at the bottom. Intoxication has great exhilaration for a while, and it fillips the blood, and it makes a man see five stars where others can see only one star, and it makes the poor man rich, and turns cheeks which are white red as roses; but what about the dreams that come after, when he seems falling from great heights, or is prostrated by other fancied disasters, and the perspiration stands on the forehead, the night dew of everlasting darkness, and he is ground under the horrible hoof of nightmares shrieking with lips that crackle with all-consuming torture? "Rejoice, O young man, in thy youth, and let thy heart cheer thee in the days of thy youth; but know thou, that for all these things God will bring thee into judgment!"

SWEET AT THE START,

horrible at the last. Go into that hall of revelry, where ungodly mirth staggers and blasphemes. Listen to the senseless gabble, see the last trace of intelligence dashed out from faces made in God's own image.

"Aha! aha!" says the roystering inebriate; "this is joy for you; fill high your cups, my boys. I drink to my wife's misery and my children's rags and my God's defiance." And he knows not that a fiend stirs the goblet in his hand and that adders uncoil from the dregs and thrust their forked tongues hissing through the froth on the rim.

PERDITION BOUGHT FOR A SIXPENCE.

The Philistines jeered and laughed and shouted at Samson. Oh, they wanted him to make sport for them, and he made sport for them! How bright and gay was the scene for a little while! After awhile the giant puts one hand against this pillar, and the other hand against this pillar, and bows himself, and three thousand merry-makers are mashed like grapes in a wine-press. Sin rapturous at the start, awful at the last.

That one Edenic transgression did not seem to be much, but it struck a blow which to this day makes the earth stagger like an ox under a butcher's bludgeon. To find out the consequences of that one sin, you would have to compel the world to throw open all its prison doors and display the crime, and throw open all its hospitals and display the disease, and throw open all the insane asylums and show the wretchedness, and open all the sepulchres and show the dead, and open all the doors of the lost world and show the damned. That one Edenic transgression stretched chords of misery across the heart of the world and struck them with dolorous wailing, and it has seated the plagues upon the air and the shipwrecks upon the tempest, and fastened like a leech famine to the heart of the sick and dying nations. Beautiful at the start, horrible at the last. Oh, how many have experienced it!

And there are those who are

VOTARIES OF PLEASURE.

Let me warn you, my brother. Your pleasure boat is far from shore, and your summer day is ending roughly, for the winds and the waves are loud voiced, and the overcoming clouds are all awrithe and agleam with terror. You are past the "Narrows," and almost outside the "Hook," and if the Atlantic take thee, frail mortal, thou shalt never get to shore again. Put back, row swiftly, swifter, swifter! Jesus from the shore casteth a rope. Clasp it quickly, now or never. Oh, are there not some of you who are freighting all your loves and joys and hopes upon a vessel which shall never reach the port of heaven? Thou nearest the breakers, one heave upon the rock. Oh, what an awful crash was that! Another lunge may crush thee beneath the spars or grind thy bones to powder amid the torn timbers. Overboard for your life, overboard! Trust not that loose plank nor attempt the move, but quickly clasp the feet of Jesus walking on the watery pavement, shouting until He hear thee, "Lord, save me, or I perish." Sin beautiful at the start—oh, how sad, how distressful at the last! The ground over which it leads you is hollow. The fruit it offers to your taste is poison. The promise it makes to you is a lie. Over that ungodly banquet the keen sword of God's judgment hangs, and there are ominous handwritings on the wall.

HIDEOUS ATTRACTIVENESS.

Observe also in this subject how repelling sin is when appended to great attractiveness. Since Eve's death there has been no such perfection of womanhood. You could not suggest an attractiveness to the body or suggest any refinement to the manner. You could add no gracefulness to the gait, no lustre to the eye, no sweetness to the voice. A perfect God made her a perfect woman to be the companion of a perfect man in a perfect home, and her entire nature vibrated in accord with the beauty and song of Paradise. But she rebelled against God's government, and with the same hand with which she plucked the fruit she launched upon the world the crimes, the wars, the tumults, that have set the universe a-wailing,

A TERRIBLE OFFSET

to all her attractiveness. We are not surprised when we find men and women naturally vulgar going into transgression. We expect that people who live in the ditch shall have the manners of the ditch; but how shocking when we find sin appended to superior education and to the refinements of social life. The accomplishments of Mary Queen of Scots make her patronage of Darnley, the profligate, the more appalling. The genius of Catharine II., of Russia, only sets forth in more powerful contrast her unappeasable ambition. The translations from the Greek and the Latin by Elizabeth, and her wonderful qualifications for a queen, made the more disgusting her capriciousness of affection and her hotness of temper. The greatness of Byron's mind made the more alarming Byron's sensuality.

Let no one who hears me this day think that refinement of manner or exquisiteness of taste or superiority of education can in any wise apologize for ill-temper, for an oppressive spirit, for unkindness, for any kind of sin. Disobedience Godward and transgression manward can give no excuse. Accomplishment heaven high is no apology for vice hell deep.

My subject also impresses me with the regal

INFLUENCE OF WOMAN.

When I see Eve with this powerful influence over Adam and over the generations that have followed, it suggests to me the great power all women have for good or for evil. I have no sympathy, nor have you, with the hollow flatteries showered upon woman from the platform and the stage. They mean nothing, they are accepted as nothing. Woman's nobility consists in the exercise of a Christian influence, and when I see this powerful influence of Eve upon her husband and upon the whole human race, I make up my mind that the frail arm of woman can strike a blow which will resound through all eternity down among the dungeons, or up among the thrones.

Of course, I am not speaking of representative women—of Eve, who ruined the race by one fruit-picking; of Jael, who drove a spike through the head of Sisera the warrior; of Esther, who overcame royalty; of Abigail, who stopped a host by her own beautiful prowess; of Mary, who nursed the world's Saviour; of Grandmother Lois, immortalized in her grandson Timothy; of Charlotte Corday, who drove the dagger through the heart of the assassin of her lover, or of Marie Antoinette, who by one look from the balcony of her castle quieted a mob, her own scaffold the throne of forgiveness and womanly courage. I speak not of these extraordinary persons, but of those who, unambitious for political power, as

WIVES AND MOTHERS

and sisters and daughters, attend to the thousand sweet offices of home.

When at last we come to calculate the forces that decided the destiny of nations, it will be found that the mightiest and grandest influence came from home, where the wife cheered up despondency and fatigue and sorrow by her own sympathy, and the mother trained her child for heaven, starting the little feet on the path to the celestial city; and the sisters by their gentleness refined the manners of the brother; and the daughters were diligent in their kindness to the aged, throwing wreaths of blessing on the road that leads father and mother down the steep of years. Need I go into history to find you illustrations? Ah no; in your own memory there was at least one such! When I come to speak of womanly influence, my mind always wanders off to

ONE MODEL,

the aged one who, twenty years ago, we put away for the resurrection. About eighty years ago, and just before their marriage day, my father and mother stood up in the old meeting-house at Somerville, New Jersey, and took upon them the vows of the Christian. Through a long life of vicissitude she lived harmlessly and usefully, and came to her end in peace. No child of want ever came to her door and was turned empty away. No one in sorrow came to her but was comforted. No one asked her the way to be saved but she pointed him to the cross. When the angel of life came to a neighbor's dwelling she was there to rejoice at the incarnation. When the angel of death came to a neighbor's dwelling she was there to robe the departed for the burial.

We had often heard her, when leading family prayers in the absence of my father, say, "O Lord, I ask not for my children wealth or honor, but I do ask that they all may be the subjects of thy comforting grace?" Her eleven children brought into the kingdom of God, she had but one more wish, and that was that she might see her long-absent missionary son; and when the ship from China anchored in New York harbor, and the long-absent one passed over the threshold of his paternal home, she said: "Now, Lord, lettest Thou thy servant depart in peace, for mine eyes have seen thy salvation." The prayer was soon answered.

It was an autumnal day very much like this when we gathered from afar and found only the house from which the soul had fled forever. She looked very natural, the hands very much as when they were employed in kindness for her children. Whatever else we forget, we never forget the look of mother's hands. As we stood there by the casket, we could not help but say: "Don't she look beautiful?" It was a cloudless day when, with heavy hearts, we carried her out to the last resting-place. The withered leaves crumbled under hoof and wheel as we passed, and the sun shone on the Raritan River until it looked like fire; but more calm and beautiful and radiant was the setting sun of that aged pilgrim's life. No more toil, no more tears, no more sickness, no more death. Dear mother! Beautiful mother!

"Sweet is the slumber beneath the sod,
While the pure spirit rests with God."

I need not go back and show you Zenobia or Semiramis or Isabella as wonders of womanly excellence or greatness, when I in this moment point to your own picture gallery of memory, and show you the one face that you remember so well, and arouse all your holy reminiscences, and start you in new consecration to God by the pronunciation of that tender, beautiful, glorious word, "Mother! mother!"

SISTERLY INFLUENCE.ToC

"And his sister stood afar off, to wit what would be done to him."—EXODUS 2:4.

Princess Thermutis, daughter of Pharaoh, looking out through the lattice of her bathing-house, on the banks of the Nile, saw a curious boat on the river. It had neither oar nor helm, and they would have been useless anyhow. There was only one passenger, and that a baby boy. But the Mayflower that brought the Pilgrim Fathers to America carried not so precious a load. The boat was made of the broad leaves of papyrus tightened together by bitumen. Boats were sometimes made of that material, as we learn from Pliny, and Herodotus, and Theophrastus.

MIRIAM'S VIGIL.

"Kill every Hebrew boy when he is born," had been Pharaoh's order. To save her son, Jochebed, the mother of little Moses, had put him in that queer boat and launched him. His sister Miriam stood on the bank watching that craft with its precious burden. She was far enough off not to draw attention to the boat, but near enough to offer protection. There she stands on the bank, Miriam the poetess, Miriam the quick-witted, Miriam the faithful, though very human, for in after time she became so mad with that very brother for marrying a woman she did not like, that she made a great family row, and was struck with leprosy.

Miriam was a splendid sister, but had her faults like all the rest of us. How carefully she watched the boat containing her brother! A strong wind might upset it. The buffaloes often found there might in a sudden plunge of thirst sink it. Some ravenous water-fowl, might swoop, and pick his eyes out with iron beak. Some crocodile or hippopotamus crawling through the rushes might craunch the babe. Miriam watched and watched until Princess Thermutis, a maiden on each side of her, holding palm leaves over her head to shelter her from the sun, came down and entered her bathing-house. When from the lattice she saw that boat she ordered it brought, and when the leaves were pulled back from the face of the child and the boy looked up he cried aloud, for he was hungry and frightened, and would not even let the princess take him. The infant would rather stay hungry than acknowledge any one of the court as mother.

AN ADROIT MAIDEN.

Now Miriam, the sister, incognito, no one suspecting her relation to the child, leaps from the bank and rushes down and offers to get a nurse to pacify the child. Consent is given, she brings Jochebed, the baby's mother, incognito, not sure of the court knowing that she was the mother, and when Jochebed arrived the child stopped crying, for its fright was calmed and its hunger appeased. You may admire Jochebed, the mother, and all the ages may admire Moses, but I clap my hands in applause at the behavior of Miriam, the faithful, brilliant, and strategic sister!

"Go home," someone might have said to Miriam. "Why risk yourself out there alone on the banks of the Nile, breathing the miasma and in danger of being attacked of wild beast or ruffian; go home!" No; Miriam, the sister, most lovingly watched and bravely defended Moses, the brother. Is he worthy her care and courage? Oh, yes; the sixty centuries of the world's history have never had so much involved in the arrival of any ship at any port as in the landing of that papyrus boat calked with bitumen. Its one passenger was to be a non-such in history. Lawyer, statesman, politician, legislator, organizer, conqueror, deliverer.

HEBREW LEGENDS.

He had such remarkable beauty in childhood that Josephus says, when he was carried along the road, people stopped to gaze at him, and workmen would leave their work to admire him. When the king playfully put his crown upon this boy, he threw it off indignantly, and put his foot on it. The king, fearing that this might be a sign that the child might yet take down his crown, applied another test. According to the Jewish legend, the king ordered two bowls to be put before the child, one containing rubies, and the other burning coals. And if he took the coals he was to live, and if he took the rubies he was to die. For some reason the child took one of the coals, and put it in his mouth, so that his life was spared, although it burned the tongue till he was indistinct of utterance ever after. Having come to manhood, he spread open the palms of his hands in prayer and the Red Sea parted to let two million five hundred thousand people escape. And he put the palms of his hands together in prayer and the Red Sea closed on a strangulated host.

UNIQUE BURIAL.

His life was unutterably grand, his burial must be on the same scale. God would let neither man nor saint nor archangel have anything to do with weaving for him a shroud or digging for him a grave. The omnipotent God left His throne in heaven one day, and if the question was asked, "Whither is the King of the Universe going?" the answer was, "I am going down to bury Moses." And the Lord took this mightiest of men to the top of a hill, and the day was clear, and Moses ran his eye over the magnificent range of country. Here, the valley of Esdraelon, where the final battle of all nations is to be fought; and yonder, the mountains Hermon, and Lebanon, and

Gerizim, and hills of Judea; and the village of Bethlehem there, and the city of Jericho yonder, and the vast stretch of landscape that almost took the old lawgiver's breath away as he looked at it.

And then, without a pang, as I learn from the statement that the eye of Moses was undimmed, and his natural force unabated, God touched the great lawgiver's eyes and they closed; and his lungs, and they ceased; and his heart, and it stopped; and commanded, saying: "To the skies, thou immortal spirit!" And then one divine hand was put against the back of Moses, and the other hand against the pulseless breast and God laid him softly down on Mount Nebo, and then the lawgiver lifted in the Almighty's arms, was carried to the opening of a cave and placed in crypt, and one stroke of the divine hand smoothed the features into an everlasting calm, and a rock was rolled to the door, and the only obsequies at which God did all the offices of priest, and undertaker, and grave-digger, and mourner were ended.

THE WORLD INDEBTED.

Oh, was not Miriam, the sister of Moses, doing a good thing, an important thing, a glorious thing when she watched the boat woven of river plants and made water-tight with asphaltum, carrying its one passenger? Did she not put all the ages of time and of a coming eternity under obligation, when she defended her helpless brother from the perils aquatic, reptilian, and ravenous? She it was that brought that wonderful babe and his mother together so that he was reared to be the deliverer of his nation, when otherwise, if saved at all from the rushes of the Nile, he would have been only one more of the God-defying Pharaohs; for Princess Thermutis, of the bathing-house, would have inherited the crown of Egypt, and as she had no child of her own, this adopted child would have come to coronation. Had there been no Miriam there would have been no Moses. What a garland for faithful sisterhood!

For how many a lawgiver, and how many a hero, and how many a deliverer, and how many a saint are the world and the Church indebted to a watchful, loving, faithful, godly sister? Come up out of the farm-houses, come up out of the inconspicuous homes! Come up from the banks of the Hudson, and the Penobscot, and the Savannah, and the Mobile, and the

Mississippi, and all the other Niles of America, and let us see you, the Miriams who watched and protected the leaders in law and medicine and merchandise and art and agriculture and mechanics and religion!

If I should ask all these physicians, and attorneys, and merchants, and ministers of religion and successful men of all professions and trades who are indebted to an elder sister for good influences, and perhaps for an education or a prosperous start, to rise, they would rise by the hundreds. God knows how many of our Greek lexicons and how much of our schooling was paid for by money that would otherwise have gone for the replenishing of a sister's wardrobe. While the brother sailed off for a resounding sphere, the sister watched him from the banks of self-denial.

THE ELDER SISTER'S POWER.

Miriam was the oldest of the family, Moses and Aaron, her brothers, are younger. Oh, the power of the elder sister to help decide the brother's character for usefulness and for heaven! She can keep off from her brother more evils than Miriam could have driven back water-fowl or crocodile from the ark of bulrushes. The older sister decides the direction in which the cradle-boat shall sail. By gentleness, by good sense, by Christian principle she can turn it toward the palace, not of a wicked Pharaoh, but of a holy God; and a brighter princess than Thermutis shall lift him out of peril, even religion, whose ways are ways of pleasantness, and all her paths are peace.

HER TOILSOME LIFE.

The older sister, how much the world owes her! Born while yet the family was in limited circumstances, she had to hold and take care of her younger brothers. And if there is anything that excites my sympathy it is a little girl lugging round a great fat child, and getting her ears boxed because she cannot keep him quiet. By the time she gets to young womanhood she is pale and worn out, and her attractiveness has been sacrificed on the altar of sisterly fidelity, and she is consigned to celibacy, and society calls her by an ungallant name, but in heaven they call her Miriam.

In most families the two most undesirable places in the record of births are the first and the last, the first because she is worn out with the cares of a home that cannot afford to hire help, and the last because she is spoiled as a pet. Among the grandest equipages that sweep through the streets of heaven will be those occupied by sisters who sacrificed themselves for brothers. They will have the finest of the Apocalyptic white horses, and many who on earth looked down upon them will have to turn out to let them, pass.

HELP TO MAKE MEN.

Let sisters not begrudge the time and care bestowed on a brother. It is hard to believe that any boy that you know so well as your brother can ever turn out anything very useful. Well, he may not be a Moses. There is only one of that kind needed for six thousand years. But I tell you what your brother will be—either a blessing or a curse to society, and a candidate for happiness or wretchedness. He will, like Moses, have the choice between rubies and living coals, and your influence will have much to do with his decision. He may not, like Moses, be the deliverer of a nation, but he may, after your father and mother are gone, be the deliverer of a household. What thousands of homes to-day are piloted by brothers! There are properties now well invested and yielding income for the support of sisters and younger brothers, because the older brother rose to the leadership from the day the father laid down to die. Whatever you do for your brother will come back to you again. If you set him an ill-natured, censorious, unaccommodating example, it will recoil upon you from his own irritated and despoiled nature. If you, by patience with all his infirmities and by nobility of character, dwell with him in the few years of your companionship, you will have your counsels reflected back upon you some day by his splendor of behavior in some crisis where he would have failed but for you.

TEASING A FAMILY CURSE.

Don't snub him. Don't depreciate his ability. Don't talk discouragingly about his future. Don't let Miriam get down off the bank of the Nile, and wade out and upset the ark of bulrushes. Don't tease him. Brothers and sisters do not consider it any harm to tease. That spirit abroad in the family is one of the meanest and most devilish. There is a teasing that is pleasurable, and is only another form of innocent raillery, but that which provokes, and irritates, and makes the eye flash with anger is to be reprehended. It would be less blameworthy to take a bunch of thorns and draw them across your sister's cheek, or to take a knife and draw its sharp edge across your brother's hand till the blood spurts, for that would damage only the body, but teasing is the thorn and the knife, scratching and lacerating the disposition and the soul. It is the curse of innumerable households that the brothers tease the sisters, and the sisters the brothers. Sometimes it is the color of the hair, or the shape of the features, or an affair of the heart. Sometimes it is by revealing a secret, or by a suggestive look, or a guffaw, or an "Ahem!" Tease! Tease! Tease! For God's sake quit it. Christ says: "He that hateth his brother is a murderer." Now, when you, by teasing, make your brother or sister hate you, you turn him or her into a murderer or murderess.

BEWARE OF JEALOUSY.

Don't let jealousy ever touch a sister's soul, as it so often does, because her brother gets more honor or more means. Even Miriam, the heroine of the text, was struck by that evil passion of jealousy. She had possessed unlimited influence over Moses, and now he marries, and not only so but marries a black woman from Ethiopia, and Miriam is so disgusted and outraged at Moses, first because he had married at all, and next, because he had practised miscegenation, that she is drawn into a frenzy, and then begins to turn white, and gets white as a corpse, and then whiter than a corpse. Her complexion is like chalk; the fact is, she has the Egyptian leprosy. And now the brother whom she had defended on the Nile comes to her rescue in a prayer that brings her restoration.

Let there be no room in all your house for jealousy, either to sit or stand. It is a leprous abomination. Your brother's success, O sisters! is your success. His victories will be your victories; for, while Moses the brother led the vocal music after the crossing of the Red Sea, Miriam, the sister, with two glittering sheets of brass uplifted and glittering in the sun, led the instrumental music, clapping the cymbals till the last frightened neigh of pursuing cavalry horse was smothered in the wave, and the last Egyptian helmet went under.

FAMILY QUARRELS.

How strong it makes a family when all the sisters and brothers stand together, and what an awful wreck when they disintegrate, quarreling about a father's will and making the surrogate's office horrible with their wrangle. Better when you were little children in the nursery that with your playhouse mallets you had accidentally killed each other fighting across your cradle, than that, having come to the age of maturity, and having in your veins and arteries the blood of the same father and mother, you fight each other across the parental grave in the cemetery.

THE ROTHSCHILDS.

If you only knew it, your interests are identical. Of all the families of the earth that ever stood together, perhaps the most conspicuous is the family of the Rothschilds. As Mayer Anselm Rothschild was about to die in 1812, he gathered his children about him, Anselm, Solomon, Nathan, Charles and James, and made them promise that they would always be united on 'Change. Obeying that injunction, they have been the mightiest commercial power on earth, and at the raising or lowering of their sceptre, nations have risen or fallen. That illustrates how much on a large scale, and for selfish purposes, a united family may achieve. But suppose that, instead of a magnitude of dollars as the object, it be doing good and making salutary impression and raising this sunken world, how much more ennobling! Sister, you do your part, and brother will do his part. If Miriam will lovingly watch the boat on the Nile, Moses will help her when leprous disaster strike.

THE FAMILY BOND.

When father and mother are gone, and they soon will be, if they have not already made exit, the sisterly and fraternal bond will be the only ligament that will hold the family together. How many reasons for your deep and unfaltering affection for each other! Rocked in the same cradle; bent over by the same motherly tenderness; toiled for by the same father's weary arm and aching brow; with common inheritance of all the family secrets; and with names given you by parents who started you with the highest hopes for your happiness and prosperity—I charge you, be loving and kind and forgiving. If the sister see that the brother never wants a sympathizer, the brother will see that the sister never wants an escort.

Oh, if the sisters of a household knew through what terrific and damning temptations their brother goes in this city life, they would hardly sleep nights in the anxiety for his salvation! And if you would make a holy conspiracy of kind words and gentle attentions and earnest prayers, that would save his soul from death and hide a multitude of sins. But let the sister dash off in one direction in discipleship of the world, and the brother flee off in another direction in dissipation, and it will not be long before they will meet again at the iron gate of Despair, their blistered feet in the hot ashes of a consumed lifetime. Alas, that brothers and sisters, though living together for years, very often do not know each other, and that they see only the imperfections and none of the virtues!

A RUSSIAN BANQUET.

General Bauer, of the Russian cavalry, had in early life wandered off in the army, and the family supposed he was dead. After he gained a fortune he encamped one day in Husam, his native place, and made a banquet, and among the great military men who were to dine, he invited a plain miller and his wife, who lived near by, and who, affrighted, came, fearing some harm would be done them. The miller and his wife were placed one on each side of the general at the table. The general asked the miller all about his family, and the miller said that he had two brothers and a sister. "No other brothers?" "My younger brother went off with the army many years ago, and no doubt was long ago killed." Then the general said: "Soldiers, I am this man's younger brother whom he thought was dead." And how loud was the cheer, and how warm was the embrace!

Brother and sister, you need as much of an introduction to each other as they did. You do not know each other. You think your brother is grouty and cross and queer, and he thinks you are selfish and proud and unlovely. Both wrong! That brother will be a prince in some woman's eyes, and that sister a queen in the estimation of some man. That brother is a magnificent fellow, and that sister is a morning in June. Come, let me introduce you: "Moses, this is Miriam." "Miriam, this is Moses." Add seventy-five per cent to your present appreciation of each other, and when you kiss good-morning; do not stick up your cold cheek, wet from the recent washing, as though you hated to touch each other's lips in affectionate caress. Let it have all the fondness and cordiality of a loving sister's kiss.

BE AGREEABLE.

Make yourselves as agreeable and helpful to each other as possible, remembering that soon you part. The few years of boyhood and girlhood will soon slip by, and you will go out to homes of your own, and into the battle with the world and amid ever-changing vicissitudes, and on paths crossed with graves, and up steps hard to climb, and through shadowy ravines. But oh, my God and Saviour, may the terminus of the journey be the same as the start, namely, at father's and mother's knee, if they have inherited the kingdom! Then, as in boyhood and girlhood days, we rushed in after the day's absence with much to tell of exciting adventure, and father and mother enjoyed the recital as much as we who made it, so we shall on the hillside of heaven rehearse to them all the scenes of our earthly expedition, and they shall welcome us home, as we say: "Father and mother, we have come, and brought our children with us." The old revival hymn described it with glorious repetition:

> "Brothers and sisters there will meet,
> Brothers and sisters there will meet,
> Brothers and sisters there will meet,
> Will meet to part no more."

I read of a child in the country who was detained at a neighbor's house on a stormy night by some fascinating stories that were being told him, and then looked out and saw it was so dark he did not dare go home. The incident impressed me the more because in my childhood I had much, the same experience. The boy asked his comrades to go with him, but they dared not. It got later and later—seven o'clock, eight o'clock, nine o'clock.

"Oh," he said, "I wish I were home!" As he opened the door the last time a blinding flash of the storm and a deafening roar overcame him. But after a while he saw in the distance a lantern, and lo! his brother was coming to fetch him home, and the lad stepped out and with swift feet hastened on to his brother who took him home, where they were so glad to greet him, and for a long time supper had been waiting. So may it be when the night of death comes and our earthly friends cannot go with us, and we dare not go alone; may our Brother, our Elder Brother, our Friend closer than a brother, come out to meet us with the light of the promises, which shall be a lantern to our feet, and then we will go in to join our loved ones waiting for us, supper all ready, the marriage supper of the Lamb!

TRIALS OF HOUSEKEEPING.ToC

"Lord, dost thou not care that my sister hath left me to serve alone? bid her therefore that she help me."—LUKE 10:40.

Yonder is a beautiful village homestead. The man of the house is dead and his widow is taking charge of the premises. This is the widow Martha of Bethany. Yes, I will show you also the pet of the household. This is Mary, the youngest sister, with a book under her arm, and her face having no appearance of anxiety or perturbation. Company has come. Christ stands outside the door and, of course, there is a good deal of excitement inside the door. The disarranged furniture is hastily put aside, and the hair is brushed back, and the dresses are adjusted as well as, in so short a time, Mary and Martha can attend to these matters.

THE WELCOME TO CHRIST.

They did not keep Christ standing at the door until they were newly appareled, or until they had elaborately arranged their tresses, then coming out with their affected surprise as though they had not heard the two or three previous knockings, saying: "Why, is that you?" No. They were ladies, and were always presentable, although they may not have always had on their best, for none of us always have on our best; if we did our best would not be worth having on. They throw open the door and greet Christ. They say: "Good morning, Master; come in and be seated."

Christ did not come alone; He had a group of friends with Him, and such an influx of city visitors would throw any country home into perturbation. I suppose also the walk from the city had been a good appetizer. The kitchen department that day was a very important department, and I suppose that Martha had no sooner greeted the guests than she fled to that room. Mary had no anxiety about household affairs. She had full confidence that Martha could get up the best dinner in Bethany. She seems to say: "Now, let us have a division of labor. Martha, you cook and I'll sit down and be good."

DIFFERENCE IN SISTERS.

So you have often seen a great difference between two sisters. There is Martha, hard working, painstaking, a good manager, ever inventive of some new pastry, or discovering something in the art of cooking and housekeeping. There is Mary, also, fond of conversation, literary, so engaged in deep questions of ethics she has no time to attend to the questions of household welfare. It is noon. Mary is in the parlor with Christ. Martha is in the kitchen. It would have been better if they had divided the work, and then they could have divided the opportunity of listening to Jesus; but Mary monopolizes Christ, while Martha swelters at the fire.

TROUBLE IN THE KITCHEN.

It was a very important thing that they should have a good dinner that day. Christ was hungry, and He did not often have a luxurious entertainment. Alas, me! if the duty had devolved upon Mary what a repast that would have been! But something went wrong in the kitchen. Perhaps the fire would not burn, or the bread would not bake, or Martha scalded her hand, or something was burned black that ought only to have been made brown; and Martha lost her patience, and forgetting the proprieties of the occasion, with besweated brow, and perhaps with pitcher in one hand and tongs in the other, she rushes out of the kitchen into the presence of Christ, saying: "Lord, dost Thou not care that my sister hath left me to serve alone?"

Christ scolded not a word. If it were scolding I should rather have his scolding than anybody else's blessing. There was nothing acerb. He knew Martha had almost worked herself to death to get Him something to eat, and so He throws a world of tenderness into His intonation as He seems to say: "My dear woman, do not worry; let the dinner go; sit down on this ottoman beside Mary, your younger sister. Martha, Martha, thou art careful and troubled about many things, but one thing is needful." As Martha throws open that kitchen door I look in and see a great many household perplexities and anxieties.

NON-APPRECIATION.

First, there is the trial of non-appreciation. That is what made Martha so mad with Mary. The younger sister had no estimate of her older sister's fatigues. As now, men bothered with the anxieties of the store, and office, and shop, or coming from the Stock Exchange, they say when they get home: "Oh, you ought to be in our factory a little while; you ought to have to manage eight, or ten, or twenty subordinates, and then you would know what trouble and anxiety are!" Oh, sir, the wife and the mother has to conduct at the same time a university, a clothing establishment, a restaurant, a laundry, a library, while she is health officer, police and president of her realm! She must do a thousand things, and do them well, in order to keep things going smoothly; and so her brain and her nerves are taxed to the utmost.

I know there are housekeepers who are so fortunate that they can sit in an arm-chair in the library, or lie on the belated pillow, and throw off all the care upon subordinates who, having large wages and great experience, can attend to all of the affairs of the household. Those are the exception. I am speaking this morning of the great mass of housekeepers—the women to whom life is a struggle, and who, at thirty years of age, look as though they were forty, and at forty look as though they were fifty, and at fifty look as though they were sixty. The fallen at Chalons, and Austerlitz, and Gettysburg, and Waterloo are a small number compared with the slain in the great Armageddon of the kitchen. You go out to the cemetery and you will see that the tombstones all read beautifully poetic; but if those tombstones would speak the truth thousands of them would say: "Here lies a woman killed by too much mending, and sewing, and baking, and scrubbing, and scouring; the weapon with which she was slain was a broom, or a sewing machine, or a ladle."

A WEARING LIFE.

You think, O man of the world! that you have all the cares and anxieties. If the cares and anxieties of the household should come upon you for one week you would be a fit candidate for Bloomingdale—I mean insane asylum. The half-rested housekeeper arises in the morning. She must have the morning repast prepared at an irrevocable hour. What if the fire will not light; what if the marketing did not come; what if the clock has stopped—no matter, she must have the morning repast at an irrevocable hour. Then the children must be got off to school. What if their garments are torn; what if they do not know their lessons; what if they have lost a hat or sash—they must be ready. Then you have all the diet of the day, and perhaps of several days, to plan; but what if the butcher has sent meat unmasticable, or the grocer has sent articles of food adulterated, and what if some piece of silver be gone, or some favorite chalice be cracked, or the roof leak, or the plumbing fail, or any one of a thousand things occur—you must be ready.

Spring weather comes, and there must be a revolution in the family wardrobe, or autumn comes, and you must shut out the northern blast; but what if the moth has preceded you to the chest; what if, during the year, the children have outgrown the apparel of last year; what if the fashions have changed. Your house must be an apothecary's shop; it must be a dispensary; there must be medicines for all sorts of ailments—something to loosen the croup, something to cool the burn, something to poultice the inflammation, something to silence the jumping tooth, something to soothe the ear-ache.

You must be in half a dozen places at the same time, or you must attempt to be.

ASSURED SYMPATHY.

If, under all this wear and tear of life, Martha makes an impatient rush upon the library or drawing room, be patient, be lenient. Oh, woman, though I may fail to stir up an appreciation in the souls of others in regard to your household toils let me assure you, from the kindliness with which Jesus Christ met Martha, that he appreciates all your work from garret to cellar; and that the God of Deborah, and Hannah, and Abigail and Grandmother Lois, and Elizabeth Fry, and Hannah More is the God of the housekeeper.

Jesus was never married that he might be the especial friend and confidante of a whole world of troubled womanhood. I blunder; Christ was married. The Bible says that the Church is the Lamb's wife, and that makes me know that all Christian women have a right to go to Christ and tell Him of their annoyances and troubles, since by His oath of conjugal fidelity He is sworn to sympathize. George Herbert, the Christian poet, wrote two or three verses on this subject:

> "The servant by this clause
>   Makes drudgery divine;
> Who sweeps a room, as for Thy laws,
>   Makes this and the action fine."

Again, there is the trial of

SEVERE ECONOMY.

Nine hundred and ninety-nine households out of the thousand are subjected to it—some under more and some under less stress of circumstances. Especially if a man smoke very expensive cigars, and take very costly dinners at the restaurants, he will be severe in demanding domestic economies. This is what kills tens of thousands of women—attempting to make five dollars do the work of seven. How the bills come in! The woman is the banker of the household; she is the president, the cashier, the teller, the discount clerk; and there is a panic every few weeks! This thirty years' war against high prices, this perpetual study of economics, this life-long attempt to keep the outgoes less than the income, exhausts millions of housekeepers.

A PREPARATION.

Oh, my sister, this is a part of the divine discipline! If it were best for you, all you would have to do would be to open the front windows and the ravens would fly in with food; and after you had baked fifty times from the barrel in the pantry the barrel, like the one of Zarephath, would be full; and the shoes of the children would last as long as the shoes of the Israelites in the wilderness—forty years. Beside that, this is going to make heaven the more attractive in the contrast. They never hunger there, and consequently there will be none of the nuisances of catering for appetites. And in the land of the white robe they never have to mend anything, and the air in that hill country makes everybody well. There are no rents to pay; every man owns his own house, and a mansion at that.

It will not be so great a change for you to have a chariot in heaven if you have been in the habit of riding in this world. It will not be so great a change for you to sit down on the banks of the river of life if in this world you had a country-seat; but if you have walked with tired feet in this world what a glorious change to mount celestial equipage; and if your life on earth was domestic martyrdom, oh, the joy of an eternity in which you shall have nothing to do except what you choose to do! Martha has had no drudgery for eighteen centuries! I quarrel with the theologians who want to distribute all the thrones of heaven among the John Knoxes and the Hugh Latimers, and the Theban Legion. Some of the brightest thrones of heaven will be kept for Christian housekeepers. Oh, what a change from here to there—from the time when they put down the rolling-pin to when they take up the sceptre! If Chatsworth Park and the Vanderbilt mansion on Fifth Avenue were to be lifted into the celestial city they would be considered uninhabitable rookeries, and glorified Lazarus would be ashamed to be seen going in and out of either of them.

THE TRIAL OF SICKNESS.

There are many housekeepers who could get along with their toils if it were not for sickness and trouble. The fact is, one-half of the women of the land are more or less invalids. The mountain lass, who has never had an ache or pain, may consider household toil inconsiderable, and toward evening she may skip away miles to the fields and drive home the cattle, and she may until ten o'clock at night fill the house with laughing racket; but oh, to do the work of life with wornout constitution, when whooping cough has been raging for six weeks in the household, making the night as sleepless as the day—that is not so easy.

Perhaps this comes after the nerves have been shattered by some bereavement that has left desolation in every room of the house, and set the crib in the garret, because the occupant has been hushed into a slumber which needs no mother's lullaby. Oh, she could provide for the whole group a great deal better than she can for a part of the group now the rest are gone! Though you may tell her God is taking care of those who are gone, it is mother-like to brood both flocks; and one wing she puts over the flock in the house, the other wing she puts over the flock in the grave.

There is nothing but the old-fashioned religion of Jesus Christ that will take a woman through the trials of home life. At first there may be a romance or a novelty that will do for a substitute. The marriage hour has just passed, and the perplexities of the household are more than atoned by the joy of being together, and by the fact that when it is late they do not have to discuss the question as to whether it is time to go! The mishaps of the household, instead of being a matter of anxiety and apprehension, are a matter of merriment—the loaf of bread turned into a geological specimen; the slushy custards; the jaundiced or measly biscuits. It is a very bright sunlight that falls on the cutlery and the mantel ornaments of a new home.

THE PROSE OF MATRIMONY.

But after a while the romance is all gone, and then there is something to be prepared for the table that the book called "Cookery Taught in Twelve Lessons" will not teach. The receipt for making it is not a handful of this, a cup of that and a spoonful of something else. It is not something sweetened with ordinary condiments, or flavored with ordinary flavors, or baked in ordinary ovens. It is the loaf of domestic happiness; and all the ingredients come down from heaven, and the fruits are plucked from the tree of life, and it is sweetened with the new wine of the kingdom, and it is baked in the oven of home trial. Solomon wrote out of his own experience. He had a wretched home. A man cannot be happy with two wives, much less six hundred; and he says, writing out of his own experience: "Better is a dinner of herbs where love is, than a stalled ox and hatred therewith."

GLORIOUS SELF-SACRIFICE.

How great are the responsibilities of housekeepers! Sometimes an indigestible article of food, by its effect upon a commander or king, has defeated an army or over-thrown an empire. Housekeepers by the food they provide, by the couches they spread, by the books they introduce, by the influences they bring around the home, are deciding the physical, intellectual, moral, eternal destiny of the race.

You say your life is one of sacrifice. I know it. But, my sisters, that is the only life worth living. That was Florence Nightingale's life; that was Payson's life; that was Christ's life. We admire it in others, but how very hard it is for us to cultivate ourselves. When in this city young Dr. Hutchison, having spent a whole night in a diphtheritic room for the relief of a patient, became saturated with the poison and died, we all felt as if we would like to put garlands on his grave; everybody appreciates that. When in the burning hotel at St. Louis a young man on the fifth story broke open the door of the room where his mother was sleeping, and plunged in amid smoke and fire, crying: "Mother! where are you?" and never came out, our hearts applauded that young man. But how few of us have the Christ-like spirit—a willingness to suffer for others!

A BARBAROUS PEDAGOGUE.

A rough teacher in a school called upon a poor, half-starved lad, who had offended against the laws of the school, and said: "Take off your coat directly, sir." The boy refused to take it off, whereupon the teacher said again: "Take off your coat, sir," as he swung the whip through the air. The boy refused. It was not because he was afraid of the lash—he was used to that at home—but it was from shame; he had no undergarment, and as at the third command he pulled slowly off his coat there went a sob through the school. They saw then why he did not want to remove his coat, and they saw the shoulder-blades had almost cut through the skin, and a stout, healthy boy rose up and went to the teacher of the school and said: "Oh, sir, please don't hurt this poor fellow; whip me; see, he's nothing but a poor chap; don't you hurt him, he's poor; whip me." "Well," said the teacher, "it's going to be a severe whipping; I am willing to take you as a substitute." "Well," said the boy, "I don't care; you whip me, if you will let this poor fellow go." The stout, healthy boy took the scourging without an outcry.[4] "Bravo," says every man—"Bravo!" How many of us are willing to take the scourging, and the suffering, and the toil, and the anxiety for other people! Beautiful thing to admire, but how little we have of that spirit! God give us that self-denying spirit, so that whether we are in humble spheres or in conspicuous spheres we may perform our whole duty—for this struggle will soon be over.

A CHRISTIAN HOUSEKEEPER.

One of the most affecting reminiscences of my mother is my remembrance of her as a Christian housekeeper. She worked very hard, and when we would come in from summer play, and sit down at the table at noon, I remember how she used to come in with beads of perspiration along the line of gray hair, and how sometimes she would sit down at the table and put her head against her wrinkled hand and say: "Well, the fact is, I'm too tired to eat." Long after she might have delegated this duty to others she would not be satisfied unless she attended to the matter herself. In fact, we all preferred to have her do so, for somehow things tasted better when she prepared them. Some time ago, in an express train, I shot past that old homestead. I looked out of the window and tried to peer through the darkness. While I was doing so one of my old schoolmates, whom I had not seen for many years, tapped me on the shoulder and said: "De Witt, I see you are looking out at the scenes of your boyhood." "Oh, yes," I replied, "I was looking out at the old place where my mother lived and died."

That night, in the cars, the whole scene came back to me. There was the country home. There was the noonday table. There were the children on either side of the table, most of them gone never to come back. At one end of the table my father, with a smile that never left his countenance even when he lay in his coffin. It was an eighty-six years' smile—not the smile of inanimation, but of Christian courage and of Christian hope. At the other end of the table was a beautiful, benignant, hard-working, aged Christian housekeeper, my mother. She was very tired. I am glad she has so good a place to rest in. "Blessed are the dead who die in the Lord; they rest from their labors, and their works do follow them."

FOOTNOTES:

[4] It may be hoped that the savage who administered it received the attention of the Board of Education. A man so grossly unjust should be in the Penitentiary.

WOMAN ENTHRONED.ToC

"There are threescore queens."—SOLOMON'S SONG 6:8.

So Solomon, by one stroke, sets forth the imperial character of a true Christian woman. She is not a slave, not a hireling, not a subordinate, but a queen; and in my text Solomon sees sixty of these helping to make up the royal pageant of Jesus. Crown and courtly attendants and imperial wardrobe are not necessary to make a queen, but graces of the heart and life will give coronation to any woman. Woman's position is higher in the world than man's, and although she has often been denied the right of suffrage, she always does vote, and always will vote, by her influence, and her chief desire ought to be that she should have grace rightly to rule in the dominion which she has already won. My chief anxiety is not that woman have other rights accorded her, but that she by the grace of God rise up to the appreciation of the glorious rights she already possesses. I shall enumerate some of those rights this morning.

I. In the first place, woman has the special and superlative right of blessing and

COMFORTING THE SICK.

What land, what street, what house has not felt the smitings of disease? Tens of thousands of sick-beds! What shall we do with them? Shall man, with his rough hand and heavy foot and impatient bearing, minister? No. He cannot soothe the pain. He cannot quiet the nerves. He knows not where to set the light. His hand is not steady enough to pour out the drops. He is not wakeful enough to be watcher. The Lord God, who sent Miss Dix into the Virginia hospitals, and Florence Nightingale into the Crimea, and the Maid of Saragossa to appease the wounds of the battlefield, has equipped wife, mother, and daughter for this delicate but tremendous mission.

You have known men who despised woman, but the moment disease fell upon them, they did not send for their friends at the bank, or their partner in business, or their worldly associates. Their first cry was, "Take me to my wife." The dissipated young man at the college scoffs at the idea of being under home influences, but at the first blast of the typhoid fever on his cheek he says,

"WHERE IS MOTHER?"

I think one of the most pathetic passages in all the Bible is the description of the lad who went out to the harvest-field of Shunem and got sun-struck, throwing his hands on his temples and crying out, "Oh, my head! my head!" and they said: "Carry him to his mother." And then the record is: "He sat on her knees till noon, and then died." It is an awful thing to be ill away from home in a strange hotel, once in a while men coming in to look at you, holding their hand over their mouth for fear they will catch the contagion. How roughly they turn you in the bed! How loudly they talk! How you long for the ministries of home!

I knew one such who went away from one of the brightest of homes for several weeks' business absence at the West. A telegram came at midnight that he was on his death-bed, far away from home. By express train the wife and daughters went westward; but they went too late. He feared not to die; but he was in an agony to live until his family got there. He tried to bribe the doctor to make him live a little while longer. He said: "I am willing to die, but not alone." But the pulses fluttered, the eyes closed, and the heart stopped. The express trains met in the midnight—wife and daughters going westward, lifeless remains of husband and father coming eastward. Oh, it was a sad, pitiful, overwhelming spectacle! When we are sick we want to be sick at home. When the time comes for us to die,

WE WANT TO DIE AT HOME.

The room may be very humble, and the faces that look into ours may be very plain; but who cares for that? Loving hands to bathe the temples; loving voices to speak good cheer; loving lips to read the comforting promises of Jesus. In the war men cast the cannon; men fashioned the musketry; men cried to the hosts, "Forward, march!" men hurled their battalions on the sharp edges of the enemy, crying, "Charge! charge!" but woman scraped the lint; woman administered the cordials; woman watched by the dying couch; woman wrote the last message to the home circle; woman wept at the solitary burial, attended by herself and four men with a spade. We greeted the generals home with brass bands and triumphal arches and wild huzzas; but the story is too good to be written anywhere, save in

THE CHRONICLES OF HEAVEN,

of Mrs. Brady, who came down among the sick in the swamps of the Chickahominy; of Annie Ross in the cooper-shop hospital; of Margaret Breckinridge, who came to men who had been for weeks with their wounds undressed, some of them frozen to the ground, and when she turned them over, those who had an arm left waved it, and filled the air with their "hurrah!"—of Mrs. Hodge, who came from Chicago with blankets and with pillows, until the men shouted: "Three cheers for the Christian-Commission! God bless the women at home!" then sitting down to take the last message: "Tell my wife not to fret about me, but to meet me in heaven; tell her to train up the boys whom we have loved so well; tell her we shall meet again in the good land; tell her to bear my loss like the Christian wife of a Christian soldier"—and of Mrs. Shelton, into whose face the convalescent soldier looked and said: "Your grapes and cologne cured me."

Men did their work with shot, and shell, and carbine, and howitzer;

WOMEN DID THEIR WORK

with socks, and slippers, and bandages, and warm drinks, and Scripture texts, and gentle strokings of the hot temples, and stories of that land where they never have any pain. Men knelt down over the wounded and said: "On which side did you fight?" Women knelt down over the wounded and said: "Where are you hurt? What nice thing can I make for you to eat? What makes you cry?" To-night, while we men are sound asleep in our beds, there will be a light in yonder loft; there will be groaning down that dark alley; there will be cries of distress in that cellar. Men will sleep, and women will watch.

II. Again, woman has a superlative right to take

CARE OF THE POOR.

There are hundreds and thousands of them in all our cities. There is a kind of work that men cannot do for the poor. Here comes a group of little barefoot children to the door of the Dorcas Society. They need to be clothed and provided for. Which of these directors of banks would know how many yards it would take to make that little girl a dress? Which of these masculine hands could fit a hat to that little girl's head? Which of the wise men would know how to tie on that new pair of shoes? Man sometimes gives his charity in a rough way, and it falls like the fruit of a tree in the East, which fruit comes down so heavily that it breaks the skull of the man who is trying to gather it. But woman glides so softly into the house of destitution, and finds out all the sorrows of the place, and puts so quietly the donation on the table, that all the family come out on the front steps as she departs, expecting that from under her shawl she will thrust out two wings and go right up toward heaven, from whence she seems to have come down.

O Christian young woman, if you would make yourself happy and win the blessing of Christ, go out

AMONG THE DESTITUTE!

A loaf of bread or a bundle of socks may make a homely load to carry; but the angels of God will come out to watch, and the Lord Almighty will give His messenger hosts a charge, saying, "Look after that woman; canopy her with your wings and shelter her from all harm;" and while you are seated in the house of destitution and suffering, the little ones around the room will whisper, "Who is she? Ain't she beautiful?" and if you will listen right sharply, you will hear dripping down through the leaky roof, and rolling over the rotten stairs, the angel chant that shook Bethlehem: "Glory to God in the highest, and on earth peace, good-will to men."

Can you tell me why a Christian woman, going-down among

THE HAUNTS OF INIQUITY

on a Christian errand, never meets with any indignity? I stood in the chapel of Helen Chalmers, the daughter of the celebrated Dr. Chalmers, in the most abandoned part of the city of Edinburgh; and I said to her, as I looked around upon the fearful surroundings of that place, "Do you come here nights to hold a service?" "Oh yes," she said, "I take my lantern and I go through all these haunts of sin, the darkest and the worst; and I ask all the men and women to come to the chapel; and then I sing for them, and I pray for them, and I talk to them." I said, "Can it be possible that you never meet with an insult while performing this Christian errand?" "Never," she said, "never."

That young woman who has her father by her side walking down the street, and an armed police at each corner, is not so well defended as that

Christian woman who goes forth on gospel work into the haunts of iniquity, carrying Bibles and bread. Some one said, "I dislike very much to see that Christian woman teaching those bad boys

IN THE MISSION SCHOOL;

I am afraid to have her instruct them." "So," said another man, "I am afraid too." Said the first: "I am afraid they will use vile language before they leave the place." "Ah!" said the other man, "I am not afraid of that. What I am afraid of is that if any of those boys should use a bad word in that presence, the other boys would tear him to pieces and kill him on the spot."

SOLICITATION OF CHARITIES.

Backed up by barrels in which there is no flour, and by stoves in which there is no fire, and by wardrobes in which there are no clothes, a woman is irresistible; passing on her errand, God says to her, "You go into that bank, or store, or shop, and get the money." She goes in and gets it. The man is hard-fisted, but she gets it. She could not help but get it. It is decreed from eternity she should get it. No need of your turning your back and pretending you don't hear; you do hear. There is no need of your saying you are begged to death. There is no need of your wasting your time, and you might as well submit first as last. You had better right away take down your cheque-book, mark the number of the cheque, fill up the blank, sign your name, and hand it to her.

There is no need of wasting time. Those poor children on the back street have been hungry long enough. That sick man must have some farina. That consumptive must have something to ease his cough. I meet this delegate of a relief society coming out of the store of such a hard-fisted man, and I say, "Did you get the money?" "Of course," she says, "I got the money; that's what I went for. The Lord told me to go in and get it, and He never sends me on a fool's errand."

III. Again I have to tell you that it is woman's specific

RIGHT TO COMFORT

under the stress of dire disaster. She is called the weaker vessel; but all profane as well as sacred history attests that, when the crisis comes, she is better prepared than man to meet the emergency. How often you have seen a woman who seemed to be a disciple of frivolity and indolence, who, under one stroke of calamity, changed to a heroine. Oh, what a great mistake those business men make who never tell their business troubles to their wives! There comes some great loss to their store, or some of their companions in business play them a sad trick, and they carry the burden all alone. He is asked in the household, again and again, "What is the matter?" but he believes it a sort of Christian duty to keep all that trouble within his own soul. Oh sir, your first duty was to

TELL YOUR WIFE

all about it. She perhaps might not have disentangled your finances or extended your credit, but she would have helped you to bear misfortune. You have no right to carry on one shoulder that which is intended for two.

There are business men here who know what I mean. There came a crisis in your affairs. You struggled bravely and long; but after a while there came a day when you said, "Here I shall have to stop," and you called in your partners, and you called in the most prominent men in your employ, and you said, "We have got to stop." You left the store suddenly. You could hardly make up your mind to pass through the street and over on the ferry-boat. You felt everybody would be looking at you, and blaming you, and denouncing you.

You hastened home. You told your wife all about the affair. What did she say? Did she play the butterfly? Did she talk about the silks and the ribbons and the fashions? No. She came up to the emergency. She quailed not under the stroke. She helped you begin to plan right away. She offered to go out of the comfortable house into a smaller one, and wear the old cloak another winter. She was one who understood your affairs without blaming you. You looked upon what you thought was a thin, weak woman's arm holding you up; but while you looked at that arm, there came into the feeble muscles of it the strength of the eternal God. No chiding. No fretting. No telling you about the beautiful house of her father, from which you brought her ten, twenty, or thirty years ago. You said, "Well, this is the happiest day of my life. I am glad I have got from under my burden. My wife don't care—I don't care."

At the moment you were utterly exhausted. God sent a Deborah to meet the host of the Amalekites, and scatter them like chaff over the plain. There are sometimes women who sit reading sentimental novels, and who wish that they had some grand field in which to display their Christian powers. Oh, what grand and glorious things they could do if they only had an opportunity! My sister, you need not wait for any such time. A crisis will come in your affairs. There will be a Thermopylæ in your own household, where God will tell you to stand. There are scores and hundreds of households in this city to-day where as much bravery and courage are demanded of women as was exhibited by Grace Darling, or Marie Antoinette, or Joan of Arc.

IV. Again, I remark, it is woman's right to

BRING TO US THE KINGDOM

of heaven. It is easier for a woman to be a Christian than for a man. Why? You say she is weaker. No. Her heart is more responsive to the pleadings of divine love. She is in vast majority. The fact that she can more easily become a Christian I prove by the statement that three-fourths of the members of the churches in all Christendom are women. So God appoints them to be the chief agencies for bringing this world back to God.

THE GREATEST SERMONS

are not preached on celebrated platforms; they are preached with an audience of two or three, and in private home life. A consistent, consecrated Christian service is an unanswerable demonstration of God's truth.

A group of rough men were assembled at a tavern one night. It came on toward morning—one or two o'clock. One man boasted that it did not make any difference what time he went home, his wife cheerfully opened the door, and provided an entertainment if he was hungry when he got home.

So they laid a wager. They said: "Now, we'll go along with you. So much shall be wagered. We'll bet so much that when you go home and make such a demand she will resist it." So they went along at two or three o'clock in the morning and knocked at the door. The door opened, and the man said to his wife, "Get us a supper." She said, "What shall I get?" He selected the articles of food. Very cheerfully were they provided, and about three or four o'clock in the morning they sat down at the table—the most cheerful one in all that presence the Christian wife—when the man, the ruffian, the villain who had demanded all this, broke into tears, and said: "I can't stand this. Oh, what a wretch I am!" He disbanded that group. He knelt down with his Christian wife and asked her to pray for the salvation of his immortal soul, and before the morning dawned they were united in the faith and hope of the Gospel.

A patient, loving, Christian demeanor in the presence of transgression, in the presence of hardness, in the presence of obduracy and crime, is an argument from the throne of the Lord Almighty, and blessed is that woman who can wield such an argument. A sailor came slipping down the ratline one night, as though something had happened, and the sailors cried, "What's the matter?" He said,

"MY MOTHER'S PRAYERS

haunt me like a ghost." Home influences, consecrated Christian home influences, are the mightiest of all influences upon the soul. There are men here to-day who have maintained their integrity, not because they were any better naturally than some other people, but because there were home influences praying for them all the time. They got a good start. They were launched on the world with the benedictions of a Christian mother. They may track Siberian snows, they may plunge into African jungles, they may fly to the earth's end, they cannot go so far and so fast but the prayers will keep up with them.

I stand before women this morning who have the eternal salvation of their husbands in their right hand. On the marriage-day you took an oath before men and angels that you would be faithful and kind until death did you part, and I believe you are going to keep that oath; but after that parting at the door of the grave, will it be an eternal separation? Is there any such thing as

AN IMMORTAL MARRIAGE,

making the flowers that grow on the top of the sepulchre brighter than the garlands which at the marriage banquet flooded the air with aroma? Yes; I stand here as a priest of the most high God to proclaim the banns of an immortal union for all those who join hands in the grace of Christ. O woman, is your husband, your father, your son away from God? The Lord demands their redemption at your hands. There are prayers for you to offer, there are exhortations for you to give, there are examples for you to make; and I say now, this morning, as Paul said to the Corinthian woman: "What knowest thou, O woman, but thou canst save thy husband?"

A man was dying, and he said to his wife: "Rebecca, you wouldn't let me have family prayers, and you laughed about all that, and you got me away into worldliness; and now I am going to die, and my fate is sealed, and you are

THE CAUSE OF MY RUIN."

O woman, what knowest thou but thou canst destroy thy husband? Are there not some here who have kindly influences at home—are there not some here who have wandered far away from God, who can remember the Christian influences in their early home? Do not despise those influences, my brother. If you die without Christ, what will you do with your mother's prayers, with your wife's importunities, with your sister's entreaties? What will you do with the letters they used to write to you, with the memory of those days when they attended you so kindly in times of sickness? Oh, if there be but just one strand holding you from floating off on that dark sea, I would just like, this morning, to take hold of that strand and pull you to the beach. For the sake of your wife's God, for the sake of your mother's God, for the sake of your daughter's God, for the sake of your sister's God, come this day and be saved.

V. Lastly, I wish to say that one of the specific rights of women is, through the grace of Christ, finally

TO REACH HEAVEN.

Oh, what a multitude of women in heaven! Mary, Christ's mother, in heaven; Elizabeth Fry in heaven; Charlotte Elizabeth in heaven; the mother of Augustine in heaven; the Countess of Huntingdon—who sold her splendid jewels to build chapels—in heaven; while a great many others, who have never been heard of on earth, or known but little, have gone into the rest and peace of heaven. What a rest! What a change it was from the small room, with no fire and one window, the glass broken out, and the aching side and worn-out eyes, to the "house of many mansions!" No more stitching until twelve o'clock at night, no more thrusting of the thumb by the employer through the work to show it was not done quite right. Plenty of bread at last. Heaven for aching heads. Heaven for broken hearts. Heaven for anguish-bitten frames. No more sitting up until midnight for the coming of staggering steps. No more rough blows across the temples. No more sharp, keen, bitter curse.

Some of you will have no rest in this world. It will be toil and struggle and suffering all the way up. You will have to stand at your door fighting back the wolf with your own hand red with carnage. But God has a crown for you.

I want you to realize, this morning, that He is now making it, and whenever you weep a tear He sets another gem in that crown, whenever you have a pang of body or soul He puts another gem in that crown, until, after a while, in all the tiara there will be no room for another splendor, and God will say to His angel, "The crown is done; let her up that she may wear it." And as the Lord of Righteousness puts the crown upon your brow, angel will cry to angel, "Who is she?" and Christ will say, "I will tell you who she is. She is the one that came up out of great tribulation, and had her robe washed and made white in the blood of the Lamb."

A BANQUET.

And then God will spread a banquet, and He will invite all the principalities of heaven to sit at the feast; and the tables will blush with the best clusters from the vineyards of God, and crimson with the twelve manner of fruits from the Tree of Life; and water from the fountains of the rock will flash from the golden tankards; and the old harpers of heaven will sit there making music with their harps; and Christ will point you out amid the celebrities of heaven, saying, "She suffered with me on earth, now we are going to be glorified together." And the banqueters, no longer able to hold their peace, will break forth with congratulation, "Hail! hail!" And there will be handwritings on the wall—not such as struck the Persian noblemen with horror, but fire-tipped fingers writing in blazing capitals of light and love and victory: "God hath wiped away all tears from all faces!"

THE OLD FOLKS' VISIT.ToC

"I will go and see him before I die."—GEN. 45:28.

Jacob had long since passed the hundred year mile-stone. In those times people were distinguished for longevity. In the centuries after persons lived to great age. Galen, the most celebrated physician of his time, took so little of his own medicine, that he lived to one hundred and forty years. A man of undoubted veracity on the witness-stand in England swore that he remembered an event one hundred and fifty years before. Lord Bacon speaks of a countess who had cut three sets of teeth, and died at one hundred and forty years. Joseph Crele, of Pennsylvania, lived one hundred and forty years. In 1857 a book was printed containing the names of thirty-seven person who lived one hundred and forty years, and the names of eleven persons who lived one hundred and fifty years.

Among the grand old people of whom we have record was Jacob, the shepherd of the text. But he had

A BAD LOT OF BOYS.

They were jealous and ambitious and every way unprincipled. Joseph, however, seemed to be an exception; but he had been gone many years, and the probability was that he was dead. As sometimes now in a house you will find kept at the table a vacant chair, a plate, a knife, a fork, for some deceased member of the family, so Jacob kept in his heart a place for his beloved Joseph. There sits the old man, the flock of one hundred and forty years in their flight having alighted long enough to leave the marks of their claw on forehead and cheek and temple. His long beard snows down over his chest. His eyes are somewhat dim, and he can see further when they are closed than when they are open, for he can see clear back into the time when beautiful Rachel, his wife, was living, and his children shook the Oriental abode with their merriment.

The centenarian is sitting dreaming over the past when he hears a wagon rumbling to the front door. He gets up and goes to the door to see who has arrived, and his long absent sons from Egypt come in and announce to him that Joseph instead of being dead is living in an Egyptian palace, with all the investiture of prime minister, next to the king in the mightiest empire of all the world!

THE NEWS WAS TOO SUDDEN

and too glad for the old man, and his cheeks whiten, and he has a dazed look, and his staff falls out of his hand, and he would have dropped had not the sons caught him and led him to a lounge and put cold water on his face, and fanned him a little.

In that half delirium the old man mumbles something about his son Joseph. He says: "You do not mean Joseph, do you? my dear son who has been dead so long. You don't mean Joseph, do you?" But after they had fully resuscitated him, and the news was confirmed, the tears begin the winding way down the cross roads of the wrinkles, and the sunken lips of the old man quiver, and he brings his bent fingers together as he says: "Joseph is yet alive. I will go and see him before I die."

It did not take the old man a great while to get ready, I warrant you. He put on the best clothes that the shepherd's wardrobe could afford. He got into the wagon, and though the aged are cautious and like to ride slow, the wagon did not get along fast enough for this old man; and when the wagon with the old man met Joseph's chariot coming down to meet him, and Joseph got out of the chariot and got into the wagon and threw his arms around his father's neck, it was an antithesis of

ROYALTY AND RUSTICITY,

of simplicity and pomp, of filial affection and paternal love, which leaves us so much in doubt about whether we had better laugh or cry, that we do both. So Jacob kept the resolution of the text: "I will go and see him before I die." And if our friends the reporters would like to have an appropriate title for this sermon, they might call it "The Old Folks' Visit."

What a strong and unfailing thing is parental attachment! Was it not almost time for Jacob to forget Joseph? The hot suns of many summers had blazed on the heath; the river Nile had overflowed and receded, overflowed and receded again and again; the seed had been sown and the harvests reaped; stars rose and set; years of plenty and years of famine had passed on; but the love of Jacob for Joseph in my text is overwhelmingly dramatic. Oh, that is a cord that is not snapped, though pulled on by many decades! Though when the little child expired the parents may not have been more than twenty-five years of age, and now they are seventy-five, yet the vision of the cradle, and the childish face, and the first utterances of the infantile lips are fresh to-day, in spite of the passage of a half century. Joseph was as fresh in Jacob's memory as ever, though at seventeen years of age the boy had disappeared from the old homestead. I found in our family record the story of an infant that had died fifty years before, and I said to my parents: "What is this record, and what does it mean?" Their chief answer was a long deep sigh. It was yet to them

A VERY TENDER SORROW.

What does that all mean? Why, it means our children departed are ours yet, and that cord of attachment reaching across the years will hold us until it brings us together in the palace, as Jacob and Joseph were brought together. That is one thing that makes old people die happy. They realize it is reunion with those from whom they have long been separated.

I am often asked as pastor—and every pastor is asked the question—"Will my children be

CHILDREN IN HEAVEN,

and forever children?" Well, there was no doubt a great change in Joseph from the time Jacob lost him, and the time when Jacob found him—between the boy seventeen years of age and the man in midlife, his forehead developed with a great business estate; but Jacob was glad to get back Joseph anyhow, and it did not make much difference to the old man whether the boy looked older, or looked younger. And it will be enough joy for that parent if he can get back that son, that daughter, at the gate of heaven, whether the departed loved one shall come a cherub or in full-grown angelhood. There must be a change wrought by that celestial climate and by those supernal years, but it will only be from loveliness to more loveliness, and from health to more radiant health. O parent, as you think of the darling panting and white in membranous croup, I want you to know it will be gloriously bettered in that land where there has never been a death and where all the inhabitants will live on in the great future as long as God! Joseph was Joseph notwithstanding the palace, and your child will be your child notwithstanding all the raining splendors of everlasting noon. What

A THRILLING VISIT

was that of the old shepherd to the prime-minister Joseph! I see the old countryman seated in the palace looking around at the mirrors and the fountains and the carved pillars, and oh! how he wishes that Rachel, his wife, was alive and she could have come there with him to see their son in his great house. "Oh," says the old man within himself, "I do wish Rachel could be here to see all this!" I visited at the farmhouse of the father of Millard Fillmore when the son was President of the United States, and the octogenerian farmer entertained me until eleven o'clock at night telling me what great things he saw in his son's house at Washington, and what Daniel Webster said to him, and how grandly Millard treated his father in the White House. The old man's face was illumined with the story until almost the midnight. He had just been visiting his son at the Capitol. And I suppose it was something of the same joy that thrilled the heart of the old shepherd as he stood in the palace of the prime-minister. It is

A GREAT DAY WITH YOU

when your old parents came to visit you. Your little children stand around with great wide open eyes, wondering how anybody could be so old. The parents cannot stay many days, for they are a little restless, and especially at nightfall, because they sleep better in their own bed; but while they tarry you somehow feel there is a benediction in every room in the house. They are a little feeble, and you make it as easy as you can for them, and you realize they will probably not visit you very often—perhaps never again.

You go to their room after they have retired at night to see if the lights are properly put out, for the old people understand candle and lamp better than the modern apparatus for illumination. In the morning, with real interest in their health, you ask them how they rested last night. Joseph in the historical scene of the text did not think any more of his father than you do of your parents. The probability is, before they leave your house they half spoil your children with kindnesses. Grandfather and grandmother are more lenient and indulgent to your children than they ever were with you. And what wonders of revelation in the bombazine pocket of the one and the sleeve of the other!

Blessed is that home where Christian parents come to visit. Whatever may have been the style of the architecture when they come, it is a palace before they leave. If they visit you fifty times, the two most memorable visits will be the first and the last. Those two pictures will hang in the hall of your memory while memory lasts, and you will remember just how they looked, and where they sat, and what they said, and at what figure of the carpet, and at what door-sill they parted with you, giving you the final good-bye. Do not be embarrassed if your father come to town and he have the manners of the shepherd, and if your mother come to town and there be in her hat no sign of costly millinery. The wife of Emperor Theodosius said a wise thing when she said: "Husband, remember what you lately were, and remember what you are, and be thankful."

By this time you all notice what

KINDLY PROVISION

Joseph made for his father Jacob. Joseph did not say: "I can't have the old man around this place. How clumsy he would look climbing up these marble stairs, and walking over these mosaics! Then, he would be putting his hands upon some of these frescoes. People would wonder where that old greenhorn came from. He would shock all the Egyptian court with his manners at table. Besides that, he might get sick on my hands, and he might be querulous, and he might talk to me as though I were only a boy, when I am the second man in all the realm. Of course, he must not suffer, and if there is famine in his country—and I hear there is—I will send him some provisions; but I can't take a man from Padan-aram and introduce him into this polite Egyptian court. What a nuisance it is to have

POOR RELATIONS!"

Joseph did not say that, but he rushed out to meet his father with perfect abandon of affection, and brought him up to the palace, and introduced him to the Emperor, and provided for all the rest of the father's days, and nothing was too good for the old man while living; and when he was dead Joseph, with military escort, took his father's remains to the family cemetery at Machpelah and put them down beside Rachel, Joseph's mother. Would God all children were as kind to their parents!

If the father have large property, and he be wise enough to keep it in his own name, he will be respected by the heirs; but how often it is when the son finds the father in famine, as Joseph found Jacob in famine, the young people make it very hard for the old man. They are so surprised he eats with a knife instead of a fork. They are chagrined at his antediluvian habits. They are provoked because he cannot hear as well as he used to, and when he asks it over again, and the son has to repeat it, he bawls in the old man's ear: "I hope you hear that!" How long he must wear the old coat or the old hat before they get him a new one! How chagrined they are at his independence of the English grammar! How long he hangs on! Seventy years and not gone yet! Seventy-five years and not gone yet! Eighty years and not gone yet! Will he ever go? They think it of no use to have a doctor in his last sickness, and go up to the drugstore and get a dose of something that makes him worse, and economize on a coffin, and beat the undertaker down to the last point, giving a note for the reduced amount which they never pay! I have officiated at obsequies of aged people where the family have been so inordinately resigned to the Providence that I felt like taking my text from Proverbs: "The eye that mocketh at its father, and refuseth to obey its mother, the ravens of the valley shall pick it out, and the young eagles shall eat it." In other words, such an ingrate ought to have a flock of crows for pall-bearers! I congratulate you if you have the honor of providing for aged parents. The blessing of the Lord God of Joseph and Jacob will be on you.

I rejoice to remember that though my father lived in a plain house the most of his days, he died in a mansion provided by the filial piety of a son who had achieved a fortune. There the octogenarian sat, and the servants waited on him, and there were plenty of horses and plenty of carriages to convey him, and a bower in which to sit on long summer afternoons, dreaming over the past, and there was not a room in the house where he was not welcome, and there were musical instruments of all sorts to regale him; and when life had passed, the neighbors came out and expressed all honor possible, and carried him to the village Machpelah and put him down beside the Rachel with whom he had lived more than half a century.

SHARE YOUR SUCCESSES

with the old people. The probability is, that the principles they inculcated achieved your fortune. Give them a Christian percentage of kindly consideration. Let Joseph divide with Jacob the pasture fields of Goshen and the glories of the Egyptian court.

And here I would like to sing the praises of the sisterhood who remained unmarried that they might administer to aged parents. The brutal world calls these

SELF-SACRIFICING ONES

by ungallant names, and says they are peculiar or angular; but if you had had as many annoyances as they have had, Xantippe would have been an angel compared with you. It is easier to take care of five rollicking, romping children than of one childish old man. Among the best women of Brooklyn and of yonder transpontine city are those who allowed the bloom of life to pass away while they were caring for their parents. While other maidens were sound asleep, they were soaking the old man's feet or tucking up the covers around the invalid mother. While other maidens were in the cotillon, they were dancing attendance upon rheumatism and spreading plasters for the lame back of the septuagenarian, and heating catnip tea for insomnia.

In almost every circle of our kindred there has been some

QUEEN OF SELF-SACRIFICE

to whom jeweled hand after jeweled hand was offered in marriage, but who stayed on the old place because of the sense of filial obligation until the health was gone and the attractiveness of personal presence had vanished. Brutal society may call such a one by a nickname. God calls her daughter, and Heaven calls her saint, and I call her domestic martyr. A half dozen ordinary women have not as much nobility as could be found in the smallest joint of the little finger of her left hand. Although the world has stood six thousand years, this is the first apotheosis of maidenhood, although in the long line of those who have declined marriage that they might be qualified for some especial mission are the names of Anna Ross, and Margaret Breckinridge, and Mary Shelton, and Anna Etheridge, and Georgiana Willetts, the angels of the battlefields of Fair Oaks, and Lookout Mountain, and Chancellorsville, and Cooper Shop Hospital: and though single life has been honored by the fact that the three grandest men of the Bible—John and Paul and Christ—were

CELIBATES.

Let the ungrateful world sneer at the maiden aunt, but God has a throne burnished for her arrival, and on one side of that throne in heaven there is a vase containing two jewels, the one brighter than the Kohinoor of London Tower, and the other larger than any diamond ever found in the districts of Golconda—the one jewel by the lapidary of the palace cut with the words: "Inasmuch as ye did it to father;" the other jewel by the lapidary of the palace cut with the words: "Inasmuch as ye did it to mother." "Over the Hills to the Poorhouse" is the exquisite ballad of Will Carleton, who found an old woman who had been turned off by her prospered sons; but I thank God I may find in my text "Over the hills to the palace."

As if to disgust us with unfilial conduct, the Bible presents us the story of Micah, who stole the eleven hundred shekels from his mother, and the story of Absalom, who tried to dethrone his father. But all history is beautiful with stories of filial fidelity. Epaminondas, the warrior, found his chief delight in reciting to his parents his victories. There goes Æneas from burning Troy, on his shoulders Anchises, his father. The Athenians punished with death any unfilial conduct. There goes beautiful Ruth escorting venerable Naomi across the desert amid the howling of the wolves and the barking of the jackals. John Lawrence burned at the stake in Colchester, was cheered in the flames by his children, who said: "O God, strengthen thy servant and keep thy promise!" And Christ in the hour of excruciation provided for His old mother. Jacob kept his resolution, "I will go and see him before I die," and a little while after we find them walking the tessellated floor of the palace, Jacob and Joseph, the prime-minister proud of the shepherd.

I may say in regard to the most of you that your parents have probably visited you for the last time, or will soon pay you such a visit, and I have wondered if they will ever visit you

IN THE KING'S PALACE.

"Oh," you say, "I am in the pit of sin!" Joseph was in the pit. "Oh," you say, "I am in the prison of mine iniquity!" Joseph was once in prison. "Oh," you say, "I didn't have a fair chance; I was denied maternal kindness!" Joseph was denied maternal attendance. "Oh," you say, "I am far away from the land of my nativity!" Joseph was far from home. "Oh," you say, "I have been betrayed and exasperated!" Did not Joseph's brethren sell him to a passing Ishmaelitish caravan? Yet God brought him to that emblazoned residence; and if you will trust His grace in Jesus Christ you, too, will be empalaced. Oh, what a day that will be when the old folks come from an adjoining mansion in heaven, and find you amid the alabaster pillars of the throne-room and living with the king! They are coming up the steps now, and the epauletted guard of the palace rushes in and says: "Your father's coming, your mother's coming!" And when under the arches of precious stones and on the pavement of porphyry you greet each other, the scene will eclipse the meeting on the Goshen highway, when Joseph and Jacob fell on each other's neck and wept a good while.

But oh, how changed the old folks will be! Their cheek smoothed into the flesh of a little child. Their stooped posture lifted into immortal symmetry. Their foot now so feeble, then with the sprightliness of a bounding roe as they shall say to you: "A spirit passed this way from earth and told us that you were wayward and dissipated after we left the world; but you have repented, our prayer has been answered, and you are here; and as we used to visit you on earth before we died, now we visit you in your new home after our ascension." And father will say, "Mother, don't you see Joseph is yet alive?" and mother will say, "Yes, father, Joseph is yet alive." And then they will talk over their earthly anxieties in regard to you, and the midnight supplications in your behalf, and they will recite to each other the old Scripture passage with which they used to cheer their staggering faith: "I will be a God to thee and thy seed after thee." Oh, the palace, the palace, the palace! That is what Richard Baxter called "The Saints' Everlasting Rest." That is what John Bunyan called the "Celestial City." That is Young's "Night Thoughts" turned into morning exultations. That is Gray's "Elegy in a Churchyard" turned to resurrection spectacle. That is the "Cotter's Saturday Night" exchanged for the Cotter's Sabbath morning. That is the shepherd of Salisbury Plain amid the flocks on the hills of heaven. That is the famine-struck Padan-aram turned into the rich pasture fields of Goshen. That is Jacob visiting Joseph at the emerald castle.

THE DOMESTIC CIRCLE.ToC

"Go home to thy friends, and tell them how great things the Lord hath done for thee."—MARK 5:19.

There are a great many people longing for some grand sphere in which to serve God. They admire Luther at the Diet of Worms, and only wish that they had some such great opportunity in which to display their Christian prowess. They admire Paul making Felix tremble, and they only wish that they had some such grand occasion in which to preach righteousness, temperance, and judgment to come; all they want is only an opportunity to exhibit their Christian heroism. Now the evangelist comes to us, and he practically says: "I will show you a place where you can exhibit all that is grand, and beautiful, and glorious in Christian character, and that is the domestic circle."

EVERY MAN'S OPPORTUNITY.

If one is not faithful in an insignificant sphere he will not be faithful in a resounding sphere. If Peter will not help the cripple at the gate of the temple, he will never be able to preach three thousand souls into the kingdom at the Pentecost. If Paul will not take pains to instruct in the way of salvation the jailor of the Philippian dungeon, he will never make Felix tremble. He who is not faithful in a skirmish would not be faithful in an Armageddon. The fact is we are all placed in just the position in which we can most grandly serve God; and we ought not to be chiefly thoughtful about some sphere of usefulness which we may after a while gain, but the all-absorbing question with you and with me ought to be: "Lord, what wilt thou have me now and here to do?"

WHAT A HOME IS.

There is one word in my text around which the most of our thoughts will this morning revolve. That word is "Home." Ask ten different men the meaning of that word, and they will give you ten different definitions. To one it means love at the hearth, it means plenty at the table, industry at the workstand, intelligence at the books, devotion at the altar. To him it means a greeting at the door and a smile at the chair. Peace hovering like wings. Joy clapping its hands with laughter. Life a tranquil lake. Pillowed on the ripples sleep the shadows.

Ask another man what home is, and he will tell you it is want, looking out of a cheerless firegrate, kneading hunger in an empty bread tray. The damp air shivering with curses. No Bible on the shelf. Children robbers and murderers in embryo. Obscene songs their lullaby. Every face a picture of ruin. Want in the background and sin staring from the front. No Sabbath wave rolling over that door-sill. Vestibule of the pit. Shadow of infernal walls. Furnace for forging everlasting chains. Faggots for an unending funeral pile. Awful word! It is spelled with curses, it weeps with ruin, it chokes with woe, it sweats with the death agony of despair.

The word "Home" in the one case means everything bright. The word "Home" in the other case means everything terrific.

I shall speak to you this morning of home as a test of character, home as a refuge, home as a political safeguard, home as a school, and home as a type of heaven.

And in the first place I remark, that home is a powerful test of character. The disposition in public may be in gay costume, while in private it is in dishabille. As play actors may appear in one way on the stage, and may appear in another way behind the scenes, so private character may be very different from public character. Private character is often public character turned wrong side out. A man may receive you into his parlor as though he were a distillation of smiles, and yet his heart may be a swamp of nettles. There are business men who all day long are mild, and courteous, and genial, and good-natured in commercial life, damming back their irritability, and their petulance, and their discontent; but at nightfall the dam breaks, and scolding pours forth in floods and freshets.

HOME MANNERS.

Reputation is only the shadow of character, and a very small house sometimes will cast a very long shadow. The lips may seem to drop with myrrh and cassia, and the disposition to be as bright and warm as a sheaf of sunbeams, and yet they may only be a magnificent show window to a wretched stock of goods. There is many a man who is affable in public life and amid commercial spheres who, in a cowardly way, takes his anger and his petulance home, and drops them on the domestic circle.

The reason men do not display their bad temper in public is because they do not want to be knocked down. There are men who hide their petulance and their irritability just for the same reason that they do not let their notes go to protest. It does not pay. Or for the same reason that they do not want a man in their stock company to sell his stock at less than the right price, lest it depreciate the value. As at some time the wind rises, so after a sunshiny day there may be a tempestuous night. There are people who in public act the philanthropist, who at home act the Nero, with respect to their slippers and their gown.

AUDUBON'S GREATNESS.

Audubon, the great ornithologist, with gun and pencil, went through the forests of America to bring down and to sketch the beautiful birds, and after years of toil and exposure completed his manuscript, and put it in a trunk in Philadelphia for a few days of recreation and rest, and came back and found that the rats had utterly destroyed the manuscript; but without any discomposure and without any fret or bad temper, he again picked up his gun and pencil, and visited again all the great forests of America, and reproduced his immortal work. And yet there are people with the ten thousandth part of that loss who are utterly unreconcilable, who, at the loss of a pencil or an article of raiment will blow as long and sharp as a northeast storm.

Now, that man who is affable in public and who is irritable in private is making a fraudulent overissue of stock, and he is as bad as a bank that might have four or five hundred thousand dollars of bills in circulation with no specie in the vault. Let us learn to show piety at home. If we have it not there, we have it not anywhere. If we have not genuine grace in the family circle, all our outward and public plausibility merely springs from a fear of the world or from the slimy, putrid pool of our own selfishness. I tell you the home is a mighty test of character! What you are at home you are everywhere, whether you demonstrate it or not.

HOME A REFUGE.

Again, I remark that home is a refuge. Life is the United States army on the national road to Mexico, a long march, with ever and anon a skirmish and a battle. At eventide we pitch our tent and stack the arms, we hang up the war cap and lay our head on the knapsack, we sleep until the morning bugle calls us to marching and action. How pleasant it is to rehearse the victories and the surprises, and the attacks of the day, seated by the still camp-fire of the home circle!

Yea, life is a stormy sea. With shivered masts, and torn sails, and hulk aleak, we put in at the harbor of home. Blessed harbor! There we go for repairs in the dry dock of quiet life. The candle in the window is to the toiling man the lighthouse guiding him into port. Children go forth to meet their fathers as pilots at the "Narrows" take the hand of ships. The door-sill of the home is the wharf where heavy life is unladen.

There is the place where we may talk of what we have done without being charged with self adulation. There is the place where we may lounge without being thought ungraceful. There is the place where we may express affection without being thought silly. There is the place where we may forget our annoyances, and exasperations, and troubles. Forlorn earth pilgrim! no home? Then die. That is better. The grave is brighter, and grander, and more glorious than this world with no tent for marchings, with no harbor from the storm, with no place of rest from this scene of greed, and gouge, and loss, and gain. God pity the man or the woman who has no home!

A POLITICAL SAFEGUARD.

Further, I remark that home is a political safeguard. The safety of the State must be built on the safety of the home. Why cannot France come to a placid republic? Ever and anon there is a threat of national capsize. France as a nation has not the right kind of a Christian home. The Christian hearthstone is the only corner-stone for a republic. The virtues cultured in the family circle are an absolute necessity for the State. If there be not enough moral principle to make the family adhere, there will not be enough political principle to make the State adhere. "No home" means the Goths and Vandals, means the Nomads of Asia, means the Numideans of Africa, changing from place to place, according as the pasture happens to change. Confounded be all those Babels of iniquity which would overtower and destroy the home. The same storm that upsets the ship in which the family sails will sink the frigate of the constitution. Jails and penitentiaries and armies and navies are not our best defence. The door of the home is the best fortress. Household utensils are the best artillery, and the chimneys of our dwelling houses are the grandest monuments of safety and triumph. No home; no republic.

AS A SCHOOL.

Further, I remark, that home is a school. Old ground must be turned up with subsoil plough, and it must be harrowed and re-harrowed, and then the crop will not be as large as that of the new ground with less culture. Now youth and childhood are new ground, and all the influences thrown over their heart and life will come up in after life luxuriantly. Every time you have given a smile of approbation, all the good cheer of your life will come up again in the geniality of your children. And every ebullition of anger and every uncontrollable display of indignation will be fuel to their disposition twenty, or thirty, or forty years from now—fuel for a bad fire a quarter of a century from this.

You praise the intelligence of your child too much sometimes when you think he is not aware of it, and you will see the result of it before ten years of age in his annoying affectations. You praise his beauty, supposing he is not large enough to understand what you say, and you will find him standing on a high chair before a flattering mirror. Words and deeds and example are the seed of character, and children are very apt to be the second edition of their parents. Abraham begat Isaac, so virtue is apt to go down in the ancestral line; but Herod begat Archelaus, so iniquity is transmitted. What vast responsibility comes upon parents in view of this subject!

Oh, make your home the brightest place on earth, if you would charm your children to the high path of virtue, and rectitude, and religion! Do not always turn the blinds the wrong way. Let the light which puts gold on the gentian and spots the pansy pour into your dwellings. Do not expect the little feet to keep step to a dead march. Do not cover up your walls with such pictures as West's "Death on a Pale Horse," or Tintoretto's "Massacre of the Innocents." Rather cover them, if you have pictures, with "The Hawking Party," and "The Mill by the Mountain Stream," and "The Fox Hunt," and "The Children Amid Flowers," and "The Harvest Scene," and "The Saturday Night Marketing."

CHEERFUL HOMES.

Get you no hint of cheerfulness from grasshopper's leap, and lamb's frisk, and quail's whistle, and garrulous streamlet, which from the rock at the mountain-top clear down to the meadow ferns under the shadow of the steep, comes looking for the steepest place to leap off at, and talking just to hear itself talk? If all the skies hurtled with tempest and everlasting storm wandered over the sea, and every mountain stream went raving mad, frothing at the mouth with mud foam, and there were nothing but simooms blowing among the hills, and there were neither lark's carol nor humming bird's trill, nor waterfall's dash, but only a bear's bark, and panther's scream, and wolf's howl, then you might well gather into your homes only the shadows. But when God has strewn the earth and the heavens with beauty and with gladness, let us take into our home circle all innocent hilarity, all brightness, and all good cheer. A dark home makes bad boys and bad girls in preparation for bad men and bad women.

Above all, my friends, take into your homes Christian principle. Can it be that in any of the comfortable homes of my congregation the voice of prayer is never lifted? What! No supplication at night for protection? What! No thanksgiving in the morning for care? How, my brother, my sister, will you answer God in the Day of Judgment, with reference to your children? It is a plain question and therefore I ask it. In the tenth chapter of Jeremiah God says He will pour out His fury upon the families that call not upon His name. O parents! when you are dead and gone, and the moss is covering the inscription of the tombstones will your children look back and think of father and mother at family prayer? Will they take the old family Bible and open it and see the mark of tears of contrition and tears of consoling promise wept by eyes long before gone out into darkness?

CHILDREN'S CURSES.

Oh, if you do not inculcate Christian principle in the hearts of your children, and you do not warn them against evil, and you do not invite them to holiness and to God, and they wander on into dissipation and into infidelity, and at last make shipwreck of their immortal soul, on their deathbed and in their Day of Judgment they will curse you! Seated by the register or the stove, what if on the wall should come out the history of your children? What a history—the mortal and immortal life of your loved ones! Every parent is writing the history of his child. He is writing it, composing it into a song, or turning it into a groan.

My mind runs back to one of the best of early homes. Prayer, like a roof, over it. Peace, like an atmosphere, in it. Parents, personifications of faith in trial and comfort in darkness. The two pillars of that earthly home long ago crumbled to dust. But shall I ever forget that early home? Yes, when the flower forgets the sun that warms it. Yes, when the mariner forgets the star that guided him. Yes, when love has gone out on the heart's altar and memory has emptied its urn into forgetfulness. Then, the home of my childhood, I will forget thee! The family altar of a father's importunity and a mother's tenderness, the voices of affection, the funerals of our dead father and mother with interlocked arms like intertwining branches of trees making a perpetual arbor of love, and peace, and kindness—then I will forget them—then and only then. You know, my brother, that a hundred times you have been kept out of sin by the memory of such a scene as I have been describing. You have often had raging temptations, but you know what has held you with supernatural grasp. I tell you a man who has had such a good home as that never gets over it, and a man who has had a bad early home never gets over it.

Again, I remark, that home is a type of heaven. To bring us to that home Christ left His home. Far up and far back in the history of heaven there came a period when its most illustrious citizen was about to absent Himself. He was not going to sail from beach to beach; we have often done that. He was not going to put out from one hemisphere to another hemisphere; many of us have done that. But he was to sail from world to world, the spaces unexplored and the immensities untraveled. No world had ever hailed heaven, and so far as we know heaven had never hailed any other world. I think that the windows and the balconies were thronged, and that the pearline beach was crowded with those who had come to see Him sail out the harbor of light into the oceans beyond.

THE EXILE.

Out, and out, and out, and on, and on, and on, and down, and down, and down He sped, until one night, with only one to greet Him, He arrived. His disembarkation so unpretending, so quiet, that it was not known on earth until the excitement in the cloud gave intimation that something grand and glorious had happened. Who comes there? From what port did He sail? Why was this the place of His destination? I question the shepherds, I question the camel drivers, I question the angels. I have found out. He was an exile. But the world has had plenty of exiles—Abraham an exile from Ur of the Chaldees; John an exile from Ephesus; Kosciusko an exile from Poland; Mazzini an exile from Rome; Emmett an exile from Ireland; Victor Hugo an exile from France; Kossuth an exile from Hungary. But this one of whom I speak to-day had such resounding farewell and came into such chilling reception—for not even an hostler came out with his lantern to help Him in—that He is more to be celebrated than any other expatriated one of earth or heaven.

HOMESICKNESS.

It is ninety-five million miles from here to the sun, and all astronomers agree in saying that our solar system is only one of the small wheels of the great machinery of the universe, turning round some one great centre, the centre so far distant it is beyond all imagination and calculation; and if, as some think, that great centre in the distance is heaven, Christ came far from home when He came here. Have you ever thought of the homesickness of Christ? Some of you know what homesickness is, when you have been only a few weeks absent from the domestic circle. Christ was thirty-three years away from home. Some of you feel homesickness when you are a hundred or a thousand miles away from the domestic circle. Christ was more millions of miles away from home than you could calculate if all your life you did nothing but calculate. You know what it is to be homesick even amid pleasurable surroundings; but Christ slept in huts, and He was athirst, and He was ahungered, and He was on the way from being born in another man's barn to being buried in another man's grave. I have read how the Swiss, when they are far away from their native country, at the sound of their national air get so homesick that they fall into melancholy, and sometimes they die under the homesickness. But oh! the homesickness of Christ! Poverty homesickness for celestial riches! Persecution homesick for hosanna! Weariness homesick for rest! Homesick for angelic and archangelic companionship. Homesick to go out of the night, and the storm, and the world's execration, and all that homesickness suffered to get us home!

THE HOME-GATHERING.

At our best estate we are only pilgrims and strangers here. "Heaven is our home." Death will never knock at the door of that mansion, and in all that country there is not a single grave. How glad parents are in holiday times to gather their children home again! But I have noticed that there is almost always a son or a daughter absent—absent from home, perhaps absent from the country, perhaps absent from the world. Oh, how glad our Heavenly Father will be when He gets all His children home with Him in heaven! And how delightful it will be for brothers and sisters to meet after long separation! Once they parted at the door of the tomb; now they meet at the door of immortality. Once they saw only through a glass darkly; now it is face to face; corruption, incorruption; mortality, immortality. Where are now all their sins and sorrows and troubles? Overwhelmed in the Red Sea of Death while they passed through dry shod.

Gates of pearl, capstones of amethyst, thrones of dominion, do not stir my soul so much as the thought of home. Once there let earthly sorrows howl like storms and roll like seas. Home! Let thrones rot and empires wither! Home! Let the world die in earthquake struggle, and be buried amid procession of planets and dirge of spheres. Home! Let everlasting ages roll with irresistible sweep. Home! No sorrow, no crying, no tears, no death. But home, sweet home, home, beautiful home, everlasting home, home with each other, home with God.

A DREAM.

One night lying on my lounge, when very tired, my children all around about me in full romp, and hilarity and laughter—on the lounge, half awake and half asleep, I dreamed this dream: I was in a far country. It was not Persia, although more than Oriental luxuriance crowned the cities. It was not the tropics, although more than tropical fruitfulness filled the gardens. It was not Italy, although more than Italian softness filled the air. And I wandered around looking for thorns and nettles, but I found that none of them grew there, and I saw the sun rise, and I watched to see it set, but it sank not. And I saw the people in holiday attire, and I said: "When will they put off this and put on workmen's garb, and again delve in the mine or swelter at the forge?" but they never put off the holiday attire.

And I wandered in the suburbs of the city to find the place where the dead sleep, and I looked all along the line of the beautiful hills, the place where the dead might most blissfully sleep, and I saw towers and castles, but not a mausoleum or a monument or a white slab could I see. And I went into the chapel of the great town, and I said: "Where do the poor worship, and where are the hard benches on which they sit?" And the answer was made me:

"WE HAVE NO POOR

in this country." And then I wandered out to find the hovels of the destitute, and I found mansions of amber and ivory and gold; but not a tear could I see, not a sigh could I hear, and I was bewildered, and I sat down under the branches of a great tree, and I said: "Where am I? And whence comes all this scene?"

And then out from among the leaves, and up the flowery paths, and across the bright streams there came a beautiful group, thronging all about me, and as I saw them come I thought I knew their step, and as they shouted I thought I knew their voices; but then they were so gloriously arrayed in apparel such as I had never before witnessed that I bowed as stranger to stranger. But when again they clapped their hands and shouted "Welcome, welcome!" the mystery all vanished, and I found that time had gone and eternity had come, and we were all together again in our new home in heaven. And I looked around, and I said; "Are we all here?" and the voices of many generations responded "All here!" And while tears of gladness were raining down our cheeks, and the branches of the Lebanon cedars were clapping their hands, and the towers of the great city were chiming their welcome, we all together began to leap and shout and sing: "Home, home, home, home!"